WILLIAMS-SONOMA

THE WORLD KITCHEN

Favorite international recipes to cook at home

General Editor **Rick Rodgers**

weldon**owen**

From spicy Thai coconut curry and hearty French beef stew to rich Mexican carnitas tacos and honeyed Greek baklava, American cooking has evolved to embrace the exciting, vibrant flavors of the cuisines of other lands.

Williams-Sonoma *The World Kitchen* is your passport to these beloved culinary traditions. This collection of more than 150 simple, mouthwatering, and authentic recipes from Italy, France, the Mediterranean, India, China, Southeast Asia, and Mexico takes you on a culinary journey around the world through an array of wonderful dishes without ever leaving your kitchen.

Cooking international cuisine might seem like a daunting proposition if you imagine recipes that are filled with hard-to-find ingredients and specialty tools or that use time-consuming techniques. But you can make authentic and familiar dishes, just like the ones you find in your favorite restaurants, with easy-to-find ingredients, simple techniques, and no specialized equipment—the recipes in this book will show you how.

Each chapter of *The World Kitchen* represents the most beloved recipes of a country or region, organized from appetizers to soups and salads to main courses to desserts. These delectable dishes were carefully chosen to feature the enticing tastes that American cooks know and love, using readily available ingredients and with easy-to-follow instructions. The selection of international dishes is far-reaching: you'll find Mediterranean cuisines such as Moroccan, Greek, and Spanish represented along with French and Italian; Indian and

Southeast Asian dishes as well as Chinese favorites; and exciting Mexican dishes beyond the usual Tex-Mex standards. Each chapter begins with a photographic medley of the flavors and ingredients inherent in each cuisine to prime your palate for the pleasures to come.

Here are appealing dishes for every occasion and type of cooking, whether it's a simple weeknight supper or a celebratory get-together with friends. Hearty one-pot meals such as fragrant Indian Chicken Biryani (page 207), succulent Chinese Tangerine Beef Stir-Fry (page 233), or savory Moroccan Chicken Tagine with Olives and Lemon (page 121) are great for feeding a crowd. In the summer, change up your standard grilled fare by making Thai Chicken Satay with peanut sauce (page 251); Grilled Steak Tacos with Avocado (page 160) and Chile-Lime Corn (page 169); or thick, juicy Florentine Steak (page 88). And there are plenty of luscious desserts to choose from for the end of the meal, whether it's a melt-in-your-mouth Panna Cotta with Berries (page 96) from Italy, a caramelized apple Tarte Tatin (page 45) from France, or a refreshing Mango Lassi (page 212) from India.

With gorgeous, colorful photography; detailed instructions; easy-to-find ingredients; and authentic flavors, these international favorites are sure to become part of your standard fare.

Rick Rodgers

French

Aioli, the famous garlic-spiked mayonnaise of Provence, is a delicious dip for vegetables or a bold spread for sandwiches.

Crudités with Aioli

4 red, yellow, or striped beets

6–8 small new potatoes

3 carrots

2 black radishes (optional)

12 small red radishes

4 ribs celery with leaves

1 cup (8 fl oz/250 ml) Aioli (page 286)

MAKES 4 SERVINGS

1 Scrub the beets and trim the top and root ends. Place the beets in a saucepan with cold water to cover by 2 inches (5 cm) and bring to a boil over medium-high heat. Reduce the heat to medium, cover, and cook until the beets are easily pierced with a fork, 50–60 minutes. Drain the beets and rinse under running cold water. When the beets are cool enough to handle, peel the skins off, halve or cut into wedges, and set aside.

2 Meanwhile, put the potatoes in another saucepan with cold water to cover by 2 inches (5 cm) and bring to a boil over medium-high heat. Reduce the heat to medium, cover, and cook until the potatoes are easily pierced with a fork, 15–20 minutes. Drain the potatoes and set aside to cool.

3 Peel the carrots, halve lengthwise, then cut into 3-inch (7.5-cm) lengths. If using, cut the black radishes into paper-thin slices. Trim some of the leaves from the red radishes, leaving a few intact. Cut the celery ribs into 3-inch (7.5-cm) lengths. Cut the cooled potatoes in half or leave whole.

4 Arrange the beets, potatoes, carrots, radishes, and celery on a platter. Put the aioli in a bowl and set it on the platter. Serve at once.

The combination of smoky bacon, nutty Gruyère cheese, and a hint of nutmeg makes this classic French quiche a favorite.

Quiche Lorraine

Quiche Dough (page 289)

4 slices thick-cut bacon

3 eggs

1 cup (8 fl oz/250 ml) heavy cream

½ cup (4 fl oz/125 ml) half-and-half

Salt and freshly ground pepper

⅛ tsp freshly ground nutmeg

¾ cup (3 oz/90 g) shredded Gruyère cheese

MAKES 6 SERVINGS

1 Preheat the oven to 375°F (190°C). Prepare the quiche dough as directed, roll it out, and use it to line a 9-inch (23-cm) tart pan. Line the dough with aluminum foil or parchment paper and fill with pie weights or dried beans. Bake until the crust is set but not browned, 12–15 minutes. Remove from the oven and lift out the foil and weights. Prick any bubbles with a fork. Return to the oven and bake until the crust is firm and barely colored, about 5 minutes longer. Transfer to a wire rack. Reduce the oven temperature to 350°F (180°C).

2 Meanwhile, in a frying pan over medium heat, cook the bacon until crisp and browned, about 8 minutes. Set aside to drain on paper towels.

3 In a bowl, stir together the eggs, cream, half-and-half, ½ tsp salt, ½ tsp pepper, the nutmeg, and half of the cheese until blended. Crumble the cooked bacon evenly over the pastry crust and pour in the egg mixture. Sprinkle the remaining cheese evenly over the top.

4 Bake until the top is puffed and lightly golden and a knife inserted into the center comes out clean, 25–30 minutes. Transfer to the wire rack and let stand for about 15 minutes. Cut into wedges and serve warm, or let cool to room temperature.

Crushing the cooked potatoes instead of puréeing them gives this simple, comforting soup a hearty, full-bodied texture.

Potato-Leek Soup

2 tbsp olive oil

2 leeks, white and tender green part, sliced crosswise

6 cups (48 fl oz/1.5 l) chicken stock, homemade (page 283) or purchased

1 lb (500 g) Yukon gold or other waxy potatoes, peeled and cut into large chunks

1 tsp minced fresh rosemary

1 bay leaf

Salt and freshly ground pepper

MAKES 4–6 SERVINGS

1 In a large saucepan over medium heat, warm the olive oil. Add the leeks and cook, stirring, until translucent, 5–6 minutes. Pour in the stock and bring to a boil. Add the potatoes, half of the minced rosemary, the bay leaf, and ¼ tsp pepper. Cover partially, reduce the heat to low, and simmer until the potatoes are tender when pierced with a fork, 15–20 minutes.

2 Remove the pan from the heat and discard the bay leaf. Using a fork or potato masher, crush the potatoes into small chunks. Season with salt.

3 Ladle the soup into warmed bowls. Sprinkle with the remaining minced rosemary, dividing it evenly. Serve at once.

French Onion Soup

8 tbsp (4 oz/125 g)
unsalted butter

¼ cup (2 fl oz/60 ml) olive oil,
plus extra for brushing

2 lb (1 kg) yellow onions,
very thinly sliced

½ tsp sugar

Salt and freshly ground pepper

1½ tsp flour

8 cups (64 fl oz/2 l)
beef stock, homemade
(page 283) or purchased

1 cup (8 fl oz/250 ml)
dry white wine

6–8 slices coarse country
bread, each about ½ inch
(12 mm) thick

2 cloves garlic, halved

2 cups (8 oz/250 g) shredded
Gruyère or Emmentaler cheese

MAKES 6–8 SERVINGS

1 Melt 6 tbsp (3 oz/90 g) of the butter with the olive oil in a large, heavy saucepan over medium heat. Stir in the onions and sauté until translucent, 4–5 minutes. Reduce the heat to low, cover, and cook until the onions are lightly golden, about 15 minutes. Uncover and sprinkle with the sugar and ½ tsp salt. Raise the heat to medium and cook uncovered, stirring often, until the onions are deep golden brown, 30–40 minutes.

2 Sprinkle the flour over the caramelized onions and cook, stirring, until the flour is lightly browned, 2–3 minutes. Stirring constantly, slowly pour in the stock. Raise the heat to high and bring to a boil. Stir in the wine and 1 tsp pepper. Reduce the heat to low, cover, and cook until the onions begin to fall apart, about 45 minutes.

3 Meanwhile, preheat the oven to 375°F (190°C). Place the bread slices on a baking sheet and toast, turning once, until dried out but not browned, about 5 minutes. Rub both sides of the bread with the garlic halves and brush both sides lightly with olive oil. Return to the oven and toast, turning once, until golden brown, 4–6 minutes total. Set aside.

4 Increase the oven temperature to 450°F (230°C). Cut the remaining 2 tbsp butter into small pieces. Place 6–8 ovenproof soup bowls on a baking sheet. Ladle the soup into the bowls, filling them to within ½ inch (12 mm) of the rim. Top each with 1 toasted bread slice, sprinkle evenly with the cheese, and dot with the pieces of butter. Bake until the cheese is melted and the soup bubbles around the edges, 15–20 minutes. Serve at once.

Endive & Apple Salad

3 oz (90 g) blue cheese

3 tbsp olive oil

2 tsp champagne vinegar

1 shallot, minced

Freshly ground pepper

6 heads Belgian endive

2 red apples, cored and cut lengthwise into thin slices

½ cup (2 oz/60 g) walnuts, toasted (page 290) and coarsely chopped

2 tbsp minced fresh chives

MAKES 4–6 SERVINGS

1 In a large bowl, combine one-third of the cheese, the olive oil, and vinegar. Using a fork, mash the cheese into the oil and vinegar to blend. Stir in the shallot and ¼ tsp pepper. Set aside.

2 Rinse and dry the endive well. Trim the stem end of each endive. Coarsely chop 3 of the heads. Slice the remaining 3 heads lengthwise into slivers about ¼ inch (6 mm) thick. Add the endive, apples, and walnuts to the bowl with the dressing and toss the salad well.

3 Divide the salad among individual salad plates. Crumble the remaining two-thirds cheese and divide among the salads. Sprinkle with the chives and serve at once.

This French-style salad is a perfect balance of salty cheese, toasted nuts, sweet apple, and bitter endive.

This beloved French salad brilliantly combines a variety of ingredients. In the spring, add artichokes or fava beans.

Niçoise Salad

½ lb (250 g) fresh tuna, or 1 can (7 oz/220 g) olive oil–packed tuna

Salt and freshly ground pepper

½ cup (4 fl oz/125 ml) plus 3 tbsp olive oil

6 baby artichokes, trimmed, halved, and choke removed (page 291; optional)

6 small, waxy potatoes

20–24 slender green beans

¼ cup (2 fl oz/60 ml) fresh lemon juice

1 tsp Dijon mustard

2 cloves garlic, crushed

6 hard-boiled eggs (page 292)

1 head butter lettuce

9 small tomatoes, cut into wedges

1 red bell pepper, seeded and cut into strips

12 olive oil–packed anchovy fillets, halved lengthwise

⅔ cup (3 oz/90 g) Niçoise olives

⅓ cup (2 oz/45 g) Cooked Fresh Fava Beans (page 287; optional)

MAKES 6 SERVINGS

1 If using fresh tuna, cut the tuna into thick slices. Season both sides of the slices with salt and pepper. In a large frying pan over high heat, warm the 3 tbsp oil. Add the tuna slices and cook, turning once, until seared, about 2 minutes total. Let cool, then cut into bite-size pieces. If using canned tuna, drain and separate into large flakes. Set aside.

2 If using artichokes, bring a saucepan three-fourths full of water to a boil. Drain the artichokes, add them to the boiling water, reduce the heat to medium, cover, and cook until the artichokes are tender when pierced with the tip of a knife, 10–15 minutes. Drain, place under running cold water until cool, and drain again. Set aside.

3 Meanwhile, put the potatoes in another saucepan with cold water to cover by 2 inches (5 cm) and bring to a boil over medium-high heat. Add 1 tbsp salt, then reduce the heat to medium, cover, and cook until the potatoes are easily pierced with a fork, 15–20 minutes. Using a slotted spoon, transfer the potatoes to a colander to drain. Let cool slightly, then cut into slices. Set aside.

4 Return the water to a boil over medium-high heat, add the green beans, and cook until tender-crisp, about 4 minutes. Drain in a colander, then rinse under running cold water. Drain again and set aside.

5 To make a vinaigrette, in a bowl, whisk together the remaining ½ cup oil, the lemon juice, mustard, and garlic. Season to taste with salt and pepper.

6 Peel and quarter the hard-boiled eggs. Line a large, wide bowl or platter with lettuce leaves. Arrange the sliced potatoes, green beans, hard-boiled eggs, tomatoes, bell pepper, anchovies, olives, and tuna on the lettuce. Add the artichokes and fava beans, if using. Drizzle with the vinaigrette and serve.

Tender spring peas are especially delicious paired with fresh mint, but other herbs, such as tarragon or basil, also work well.

Peas with
Romaine & Mint

2 lb (1 kg) fresh English peas in the pod

½ head romaine lettuce

1 tbsp unsalted butter

2 tbsp minced shallots

½ cup (4 fl oz/125 ml) chicken stock, homemade (page 283) or purchased

Salt and freshly ground pepper

¼ cup (⅓ oz/10 g) minced fresh mint

MAKES 4 SERVINGS

1 Shell the peas; you should have about 2 cups (10 oz/315 g). Cut the lettuce crosswise into very thin strips.

2 Melt the butter in a large saucepan over medium-high heat. Add the shallots and sauté until translucent, about 1 minute. Add the peas, lettuce, and stock; cover and cook until the peas are tender to the bite and the lettuce has wilted, about 5 minutes. Season to taste with salt and pepper. Stir in the mint. Transfer to a serving bowl and serve at once.

Here, meaty sea bass pairs with tender artichokes, which are abundant in spring and fall. Briny olives add flavorful punch.

Baked Sea Bass with Artichokes & Olives

2 lemons, halved

16 small artichokes

3 tbsp olive oil

1 clove garlic, minced

¼ cup (2 fl oz/60 ml) chicken stock, homemade (page 283) or purchased

3 tbsp dry white wine

¼ cup (1½ oz/45 g) Niçoise olives

1 tsp *each* minced fresh thyme and fresh flat-leaf parsley

Salt and freshly ground pepper

4 sea bass fillets, each about ⅓ lb (155 g) and 1 inch (2.5 cm) thick

MAKES 4 SERVINGS

1 Preheat the oven to 400°F (200°C). Fill a large bowl with water. Squeeze the juice of 1 lemon into the water and add the spent lemon halves to the water. Working with 1 artichoke at a time, trim the stem even with the base. Snap off the small, tough leaves around the base. Cut off the upper third of the artichoke. Rub the cut surface with 1 of the remaining lemon halves. Continue to peel back and snap off the layers of leaves until you reach the tender, pale inner leaves. If the choke in the center has prickly tips, scoop it out with a spoon; if it is just furry, leave it intact, it will be edible when cooked. Quarter or halve the artichoke lengthwise and drop it into the lemon water. Repeat with the remaining artichokes and lemon. When all of the artichokes have been trimmed, drain and pat dry with paper towels.

2 In a flameproof baking dish over medium heat, warm the olive oil. Add the garlic and artichokes and sauté until the artichokes begin to soften and turn golden, 5–6 minutes. Stir in the stock, wine, olives, thyme, parsley, ½ tsp salt, and ½ tsp pepper. Nestle the sea bass fillets into the dish in an even layer. Cover with aluminum foil, transfer to the oven, and bake until the base of an artichoke is easily pierced with a fork and the fish is opaque throughout, 15–20 minutes.

3 Serve directly from the baking dish or, using a slotted spoon, transfer the fish to a warmed platter. Spoon the artichokes and olives around the fish, spoon some of the sauce over the top, and serve at once.

This delicate white wine and citrus sauce enhances the sweet, briny flavor of the scallops without overwhelming them.

Scallops in Tangerine Sauce

12 sea scallops, about 1½ lb (750 g) total weight

¼ cup (1 oz/30 g) cornstarch

Salt and freshly ground pepper

2 tbsp unsalted butter

2 tsp olive oil

1 tbsp fresh tangerine juice

4 tbsp (2 fl oz/60 ml) Sauvignon Blanc or other crisp white wine

Frisée or other greens (optional)

MAKES 3–4 SERVINGS

1 Pat the scallops dry with paper towels. On a large plate, combine the cornstarch, 1 tsp salt, and ½ tsp pepper. Lightly dust the scallops all over with the cornstarch mixture, shaking off the excess.

2 Melt ½ tbsp of the butter with the olive oil in a frying pan over medium-high heat. Add the scallops and cook, turning once, until seared on both sides, about 4 minutes total. Add the tangerine juice and 2 tbsp of the wine and deglaze the pan, scraping the bottom with a wooden spoon to dislodge any browned bits. Reduce the heat to low, add 3 tbsp water, cover, and cook until the scallops are just opaque, 2–3 minutes. Using a slotted spoon, transfer the scallops to a plate and cover loosely with aluminum foil.

3 Raise the heat to high, add the remaining 2 tbsp wine to the pan, and deglaze again, scraping the bottom to dislodge any browned bits. Cook until the liquid is reduced to about 3 tbsp, about 2 minutes. Add the remaining 1½ tbsp butter and stir until it has melted, about 2 minutes.

4 Divide the scallops and frisée, if using, among warmed individual plates. Drizzle with the tangerine sauce and serve at once.

Croques Monsieur

8 thick slices brioche
or sandwich bread

4 tbsp (2 oz/60 g) unsalted
butter, at room temperature

8 thin slices ham

⅓ cup (1½ oz/45 g) flour

Salt

⅛ tsp cayenne pepper

1½ cups (12 fl oz/375 ml)
whole milk

¾ cup (3 oz/90 g) shredded
Gruyère cheese

MAKES 4 SERVINGS

1 Spread one side of each slice of bread with butter, using 2 tbsp total. Lay 2 slices of ham on the unbuttered side of each of 4 slices of bread. Cover with the remaining 4 bread slices, placing the buttered sides up.

2 Melt the remaining 2 tbsp butter in a saucepan over medium heat. Remove the pan from the heat and whisk in the flour, 1½ tsp salt, and the cayenne. Return the pan to medium heat and gradually whisk in the milk. Reduce the heat to low and cook, stirring, until thickened, about 15 minutes. Stir in ¼ cup (1 oz/30 g) of the cheese and remove from the heat.

3 Preheat the broiler and line a baking sheet with foil. Warm a large frying pan over medium heat. Working in batches if necessary, place the sandwiches in the pan and cook, turning once, until golden, about 8 minutes total. Transfer the sandwiches to the prepared baking sheet. Spoon about ¼ cup (2 fl oz/60 ml) of the cheese sauce over each sandwich. Top the sandwiches with the remaining ½ cup (2 oz/60 g) cheese, dividing it evenly. Broil the sandwiches until the sauce bubbles and the cheese is golden, 4–5 minutes. Transfer the sandwiches to warmed plates, cut each in half, and serve at once.

These gooey cheese sandwiches are true comfort food, French style. For a *croque madame*, top with a fried egg.

Roast Pork with Apples

2 pork tenderloins, each about ¾ lb (375 g)

Salt and freshly ground pepper

1 tsp fresh thyme leaves

1 tbsp unsalted butter, plus extra as needed

1 tbsp olive oil

2 sweet apples such as Golden Delicious, peeled, cored, and sliced ½ inch (12 mm) thick

½ cup (4 fl oz/125 ml) Calvados, hard apple cider, or white wine

¼ cup (2 oz/60 g) crème fraîche or sour cream

MAKES 4–6 SERVINGS

1 Preheat the oven to 450°F (230°C). Sprinkle the pork tenderloins all over with 1 tsp salt, ½ tsp pepper, and the thyme. Melt the 1 tbsp butter with the olive oil in an ovenproof frying pan over medium-high heat. Add the tenderloins and sear, turning once, until browned, about 6 minutes total. Transfer the frying pan to the oven and roast until a thermometer inserted into the middle of a tenderloin registers 145°F (63°C), 12–15 minutes. Transfer the pork to a carving board and cover loosely with aluminum foil.

2 While the pork is resting, place the frying pan over medium-high heat. Add the apples and sauté, adding more butter as needed, until soft, about 5 minutes. Using a slotted spoon, transfer the apples to a plate. Add the Calvados to the pan and deglaze, scraping the bottom with a wooden spoon to dislodge any browned bits. Stir in the crème fraîche, reduce the heat to low, then stir in the apple slices.

3 Cut the pork into slices ½ inch (12 mm) thick and arrange on warmed individual plates. Spoon the apple mixture over the top and serve at once.

Roast pork paired with apples and crème fraîche make a hearty meal reminiscent of Normandy.

In this iconic dish, long, slow cooking in red wine with herbs produces tender chicken and vegetables deeply imbued with flavor.

Coq au Vin

4 tbsp (2 oz/60 g) unsalted butter

6 slices thick-cut bacon, cut into 1-inch (2.5-cm) pieces

12 thawed frozen pearl onions

1 chicken, 4–5 lb (2–2.5 kg), cut into 8 serving pieces (page 293)

1 tbsp flour

2 tbsp brandy

1³⁄₄ cups (14 fl oz/430 ml) Burgundy or other medium-bodied red wine

3 sprigs fresh thyme

3 sprigs fresh flat-leaf parsley

1 bay leaf

Salt and freshly ground pepper

½ lb (250 g) button mushrooms, halved

MAKES 4–6 SERVINGS

1 In a large, wide, heavy saucepan or Dutch oven over medium-low heat, melt 3 tbsp of the butter. Add the bacon and onions, and cook, stirring, until lightly browned, about 10 minutes. Using a slotted spoon, transfer the bacon and onions to a plate. Add the chicken to the pan, raise the heat to medium-high, and cook, turning as needed, until the chicken starts to brown, about 8 minutes. Sprinkle the chicken with the flour and cook, turning occasionally, until golden brown all over, about 5 minutes.

2 Remove the saucepan from the heat and pour the brandy over the chicken. Using a long match, ignite the brandy and let the flames subside. Return the bacon and onions to the pan and place over medium heat. Add 1 cup (8 fl oz/250 ml) of the wine and deglaze the pan, scraping the bottom with a wooden spoon to dislodge any browned bits. Add the remaining ³⁄₄ cup (6 fl oz/180 ml) wine, the thyme, parsley, bay leaf, ½ tsp salt, and 1 tsp pepper, reduce the heat to low, cover, and simmer, stirring occasionally, until the chicken is opaque throughout, 45–60 minutes.

3 Meanwhile, melt the remaining 1 tbsp butter in a frying pan over medium-high heat. Add the mushrooms and sauté just until lightly golden, 5–7 minutes. Remove from the heat and set aside. About 15 minutes before the chicken is done, add the mushrooms to the chicken.

4 Using a slotted spoon, transfer the chicken, onions, mushrooms, and bacon to a bowl. Using a spoon, skim off the fat from the surface of the pan juices. Raise the heat to high, bring to a boil, and cook until the liquid has thickened and reduced by nearly half, about 5 minutes. Return the chicken, onions, mushrooms, and bacon to the pan. Reduce the heat to low and cook, stirring, until heated through, 3–4 minutes. Serve the coq au vin directly from the pan or transfer to a warmed serving dish.

The success of this simple, rustic dish lies in slowly simmering the ingredients until the meat is fork-tender.

Burgundy Beef Stew

8 tbsp (2½ oz/75 g) flour

Salt and freshly ground pepper

3–4 lb (1.5–2 kg) beef chuck, cut into cubes

2 slices thick-cut bacon, diced

2 carrots, sliced

2 ribs celery, sliced

1 yellow onion, diced

1 lb (500 g) thawed frozen pearl onions

1 tsp peppercorns

1 bottle (24 fl oz/750 ml) Burgundy or other medium-bodied red wine

1 can (28 oz/875 g) diced tomatoes, drained

1 cup (8 fl oz/250 ml) beef stock, homemade (page 283) or purchased

1 tbsp tomato paste

2 tbsp unsalted butter

½ lb (8 oz/250 g) cremini or button mushrooms, sliced

MAKES 6–8 SERVINGS

1 In a shallow bowl, stir together 3 tbsp of the flour, 1 tsp salt, and 1 tsp pepper. Turn the beef pieces in the seasoned flour, shaking off any excess.

2 Preheat the oven to 350°F (180°C). Have ready a plate lined with paper towels. In a Dutch oven or large, heavy pot over medium heat, sauté the bacon until it renders most of its fat, 4–5 minutes. Using a slotted spoon, transfer the bacon to the paper towels and set aside. Working in batches if necessary, cook the beef in the rendered bacon fat, turning frequently, until browned on all sides, about 10 minutes. Using the slotted spoon, transfer the beef to another plate and set aside.

3 Add the carrots, celery, yellow onion, pearl onions, and peppercorns to the pot. Cook over medium-high heat, stirring often, until the onions and carrots begin to brown, about 5 minutes. Pour in the wine and deglaze the pot, scraping the bottom with a wooden spoon to dislodge any browned bits. Stir in the tomatoes and stock and bring to a boil. Stir in the remaining 5 tbsp (1½ oz/45 g) flour and the tomato paste and cook, stirring often, until the mixture has thickened, about 1 minute. Return the beef and bacon to the pot. Season with salt and pepper. Cover, transfer the pot to the oven and cook, stirring occasionally, until the meat is very tender, about 2 hours.

4 When the stew is nearly ready, melt the butter in a frying pan over medium-high heat. Add the mushrooms and cook, stirring often, until they release their moisture and become tender and brown, about 5 minutes. Add the mushrooms to the stew just before serving. Divide the stew among warmed shallow bowls and serve at once.

Steak Frites

4 or 5 russet potatoes,
peeled, cut into strips
¼ inch (6 mm) thick, and
immersed in cold water

Canola or peanut oil
for deep-frying

4 rib-eye steaks, each about
½ inch (12 mm) thick

2 tbsp minced fresh thyme

Coarse salt and freshly
ground pepper

MAKES 4 SERVINGS

1 Drain the potatoes and thoroughly pat dry with paper towels. Line a large plate with paper towels. Pour oil to a depth of 4 inches (10 cm) in a deep, heavy frying pan and heat to 350°F (180°C) on a deep-frying thermometer. Working in batches, carefully add about one-fourth of the potatoes to the hot oil and fry until they form a white crust but do not brown, about 2 minutes. Using a slotted spoon, transfer the potatoes to the paper towels to drain. Repeat with the remaining potatoes, allowing the oil to return to 350°F before adding the next batch. Let the potatoes rest for at least 5 minutes or up to 4 hours before frying again.

2 Sprinkle both sides of each steak with the thyme and pepper. Sprinkle about 1½ tsp coarse salt evenly over the bottom of a large frying pan and place over high heat until a drop of water sizzles upon contact, 1–2 minutes. Add the steaks and cook, turning once, until done to your liking, 4–5 minutes total for medium-rare. Transfer to a warmed platter and cover loosely with aluminum foil. Add ⅓ cup (3 fl oz/80 ml) water to the pan, scraping the bottom with a wooden spoon to dislodge any browned bits. Pour the sauce into a pitcher and set aside while you fry the potatoes a second time.

3 Working in batches, fry the potatoes again, reheating the oil to 375°F (190°C) and repeating the same process, until the potatoes form a golden crust, about 3 minutes. Transfer to fresh paper towels to drain.

4 Transfer the steaks to individual plates and pour the pan sauce over. Sprinkle the fries with salt, divide among the plates, and serve at once.

Spring Veal Stew

3 lb (1.5 kg) boneless veal shoulder, cut into cubes

Salt and freshly ground pepper

2 tbsp unsalted butter

1 tbsp olive oil

6 shallots, minced

2 oz (60 g) prosciutto, minced

½ cup (4 fl oz/125 ml) dry white wine

1 cup (8 fl oz/250 ml) chicken stock, homemade (page 283) or purchased

3 sprigs fresh thyme

2 large carrots, diced

1 bunch asparagus, tough ends trimmed and stalks cut into 1-inch (2.5-cm) pieces

1 cup (5 oz/155 g) fresh or frozen peas

1 cup (8 fl oz/250 ml) heavy cream

MAKES 8–12 SERVINGS

1 Place the veal in a large bowl. Sprinkle with 1 tsp salt and ½ tsp pepper and toss to coat evenly. In a Dutch oven or large, heavy pot over medium-high heat, melt the butter with the olive oil. Working in batches to avoid overcrowding, sauté the veal until evenly browned on all sides, 5–7 minutes. Transfer the veal to a bowl and set aside.

2 Add the shallots and prosciutto to the pot and sauté over medium-high heat for about 1 minute. Pour in the wine and deglaze the pot, scraping the bottom with a wooden spoon to dislodge any browned bits. Add the stock and bring to a boil.

3 Add the veal and any accumulated juices to the pot. Tuck the thyme sprigs among the veal, then cover and cook over very low heat for 1½ hours. Add the carrots, cover, and cook until the carrots are almost tender, about 20 minutes. Add the asparagus and peas and continue to cook, covered, until the vegetables are tender, about 10 minutes longer. Stir in the cream and cook until the sauce is heated through, about 5 minutes. Season to taste with salt and pepper. Divide the stew among warmed bowls and serve at once.

Tender veal combines with spring vegetables in this delicately-flavored and tempting seasonal stew.

Herbes de Provence, a blend of lavender, thyme, and rosemary, gives roasted lamb the flavors of southern France.

Herb-Roasted Lamb
with Potatoes

Butter for greasing

2½ lb (1.25 kg) russet potatoes, thinly sliced

1½ lb (750 g) large yellow onions, thinly sliced

1½ cups (12 fl oz/375 ml) beef stock, homemade (page 283) or purchased, plus extra as needed

1½ tbsp *herbes de Provence*

Salt and freshly ground pepper

1 bone-in leg of lamb, about 5½ lb (2.75 kg)

3–4 cloves garlic, cut into thin slivers

1 tbsp olive oil

MAKES 6–8 SERVINGS

1 Preheat the oven to 375°F (190°C). Generously butter a roasting pan. In a saucepan over medium-high heat, combine the potatoes, onions, and stock and bring to a boil. Reduce the heat to low and simmer until the potatoes are tender-crisp, about 5 minutes. Transfer the potato mixture to the prepared roasting pan.

2 Meanwhile, in a small bowl, combine the *herbes de Provence*, 1 tsp salt, and 1 tsp pepper. Using a sharp paring knife, make 20–25 slits, each about 1 inch (2.5 cm) deep, all over the lamb. Insert the garlic slivers into the slits. Rub the lamb all over with the olive oil, then with the herb mixture.

3 Place the lamb on top of the potatoes and onions. Roast until an instant-read thermometer inserted into the thickest part of the leg away from the bone registers 125–130°F (52–54°C) for medium-rare or 135–140°F (57–60°C) for medium, 1–1½ hours. If the potatoes get too dry during cooking, ladle some of the remaining stock into the pan. Remove from the oven and turn the oven off. Transfer the lamb to a carving board, cover loosely with aluminum foil, and let stand for 10–15 minutes. Return the vegetables to the oven to keep warm.

4 Cut the lamb across the grain into thin slices. Arrange on a platter with the potatoes and onions. Serve at once.

A golden, cheese-topped crust conceals creamy potatoes in this warming Alpine dish. Serve with roast pork or lamb.

Potato Gratin

1 clove garlic, crushed

2 tbsp unsalted butter, cut into small pieces, plus extra as needed

2 lb (1 kg) russet potatoes, peeled

Salt and freshly ground pepper

2 tsp minced fresh thyme, or 1 tsp dried thyme

¼ lb (125 g) Gruyère or Swiss cheese, shredded

1 cup (8 fl oz/250 ml) whole milk

MAKES 6 SERVINGS

1 Preheat the oven to 425°F (220°C). Rub a flameproof baking dish with the garlic, then coat it lightly with butter.

2 Using the thin slicing blade on a mandoline or a sharp knife, cut the potatoes into slices about ⅛ inch (3 mm) thick. Arrange half of the potato slices in a single layer in the prepared baking dish, overlapping them slightly. Sprinkle evenly with ½ tsp salt, ½ tsp pepper, half of the thyme, and half of the cheese. Dot with half of the butter pieces. Arrange the remaining half of the potato slices in an even layer on top and sprinkle with ½ tsp salt, ½ tsp pepper, and the remaining thyme. Sprinkle evenly with the remaining cheese and butter pieces.

3 In a small saucepan over medium-high heat, bring the milk to a boil. Remove from the heat and pour over the potato slices. Place the baking dish over medium-low heat and cook just until the milk begins to simmer, then transfer to the oven.

4 Cook until the potatoes are easily pierced with a fork, the milk has been absorbed, and the top is golden brown, 35–45 minutes. Transfer the dish to a wire rack and let stand for 5 minutes. Serve at once.

Summer Ratatouille

2 tsp olive oil

2 small yellow onions, chopped

2 eggplants, cut into cubes

4 cloves garlic, minced

2 zucchini, cut into cubes

2 large red, green, or yellow bell peppers, chopped

8–10 large, ripe, juicy tomatoes, peeled and seeded (page 290), then chopped

3 sprigs fresh thyme

1 sprig fresh rosemary

1 bay leaf

Salt and freshly ground pepper

¼ cup (⅓ oz/10 g) minced fresh basil

MAKES 10 SERVINGS

1 In a large, heavy saucepan over medium heat, warm the olive oil. Reduce the heat to medium-low, add the onions, and sauté until translucent, about 2 minutes. Add the eggplants and garlic and cook, stirring frequently, until the eggplants are slightly softened, 3–4 minutes. Add the zucchini and bell peppers and cook, stirring, until softened, 4–5 minutes longer. Add the tomatoes, thyme, rosemary, bay leaf, ½ tsp salt, and ½ tsp pepper and cook, stirring, for 2–3 minutes longer.

2 Cover, reduce the heat to low, and cook, stirring occasionally, until the vegetables are soft and have somewhat blended together, about 40 minutes. Stir in the basil and remove from the heat.

3 Transfer the ratatouille to a serving bowl or individual bowls. Serve warm or at room temperature.

Southern French cooks eagerly await the fresh and flavorful basil, tomatoes, peppers, zucchini, and eggplants of summer to make this classic dish.

Golden Leek Gratin

6 tbsp (3 oz/90 g)
unsalted butter

2 tbsp minced shallots

6–8 leeks, about 3 lb (1.5 kg)
total weight, white and tender
green parts, chopped

Salt and ground white pepper

2 cups (16 fl oz/500 ml) whole
milk, plus extra as needed

3 tbsp flour

¼ tsp cayenne pepper

½ cup (2 oz/60 g) shredded
Gruyère cheese

½ cup (1 oz/30 g)
fresh bread crumbs

MAKES 6 SERVINGS

1 Preheat the oven to 400°F (200°C). Melt 2 tbsp of the butter in a frying pan over medium-high heat. Add the shallots, leeks, ½ tsp salt, and ½ tsp white pepper. Reduce the heat to medium and cook, stirring often, until the leeks are translucent and soft, about 15 minutes. Set aside.

2 In a small saucepan over medium heat, warm the milk until small bubbles appear around the edge of the pan. Cover and remove from the heat.

3 In a saucepan over medium-high heat, melt 3 tbsp of the butter. Remove from the heat and whisk in the flour, cayenne, ½ tsp salt, and ¼ tsp white pepper to make a roux. Return the pan to medium-low heat, slowly whisk in the hot milk, and simmer, stirring, until the sauce thickens, about 15 minutes. If the sauce is too thin, increase the heat; if it is too thick, whisk in a little more milk. Stir in the leek mixture.

4 Pour the mixture into a baking or gratin dish. Sprinkle evenly with the cheese and bread crumbs and dot with the remaining 1 tbsp butter. Bake until the top is golden and the gratin is bubbly, 20–30 minutes. Serve at once.

This hearty side dish also works well as a main course. Serve it with a green salad to round out the meal.

A few simple ingredients combine to make this spectacular caramelized apple tart. Use purchased puff pastry to save time.

Tarte Tatin

Flour for dusting

1 sheet puff pastry, thawed if frozen

½ cup (4 oz/125 g) unsalted butter, at room temperature

½ cup (4 oz/125 g) sugar

10 or 11 tart-sweet apples, such as Gala or Pink Lady, peeled, halved, and cored

MAKES 6–8 SERVINGS

1 On a lightly floured work surface, roll out the puff pastry until it is ¼ inch (6 mm) thick. Invert a 9-inch (23-cm) cast-iron frying pan or flameproof baking dish on top of the pastry. Using a small knife, cut a circle of dough the same size as the top of the pan. Line a baking sheet with aluminum foil. Place the pastry round on the foil, cover with another piece of foil, and refrigerate until ready to use.

2 Preheat the oven to 375°F (190°C). Heavily coat the bottom and sides of the pan with the butter and sprinkle with the sugar.

3 Arrange the apple halves, slightly tilted, in a concentric circle in the pan, packing them in as tightly as you can. Place 4 or 5 halves in the center. Place the pan over medium heat and cook until the pan juices color and bubble and the apples begin to soften, 20–25 minutes.

4 Transfer the pan to the oven and bake until the apples darken in color and are soft when pierced with a fork, 20–25 minutes. Remove from the oven and cover with the chilled pastry round. Return to the oven and bake until the pastry is puffed and golden, about 25 minutes longer.

5 Remove from the oven. Run a knife along the edge of the pan to loosen the tart. Place a large plate over the top of the pan and, using potholders, carefully invert the plate and pan together, then lift off the pan to unmold the tart. Replace any apple pieces that have stuck to the pan. Serve warm or at room temperature.

Anointed with brandy and orange-flavored liqueur before being flambéed, these crêpes are both dramatic and utterly delicious.

Crêpes Suzette

4 eggs

1¾ cups (14 fl oz/430 ml) whole milk, plus extra as needed

1 tsp sugar

½ tsp salt

⅓ cup (2 oz/60 g) flour

3 tbsp unsalted butter, or as needed

Suzette Butter (page 289)

6 tbsp (3 fl oz/90 ml) brandy

3 tbsp Grand Marnier

Thin strips of orange zest for garnish (optional)

MAKES 6 SERVINGS

1 In a blender, combine the eggs and the 1¾ cups milk. Mix on medium-high speed. Add the sugar, salt, and flour and blend on medium-high speed until well combined. Cover and refrigerate for at least 2 hours.

2 When ready to cook, stir the batter; it should be the consistency of heavy cream. If it is too thick, thin with a little more milk. Heat a 12-inch (30-cm) crêpe pan or nonstick frying pan over medium heat. Add 1 tsp of the butter and tilt the pan to coat the bottom with the butter as it melts. Ladle about ¼ cup (2 fl oz/60 ml) of the batter into the pan, tilting and swirling the pan to coat the bottom with the batter. Pour any excess batter back into the bowl. Cook until the edges dry and separate slightly from the pan, 30–45 seconds. Using a spatula, turn the crêpe and cook for just a few seconds. Transfer to a warmed plate and cover with aluminum foil to keep warm. Repeat with the remaining batter, adding a little more butter to the pan as needed. You should have about 12 crêpes.

3 In a frying pan over medium-high heat, melt 4 tbsp (2 oz/60 g) of the Suzette Butter and add 4 crêpes to the pan. Using 2 forks, turn the crêpes in the butter to coat, then fold each into fourths and nestle them in the pan. Add 2 tbsp of the brandy and 1 tbsp of the Grand Marnier. Remove from the heat and, using a long match, carefully ignite the brandy and spoon the sauce over the crêpes until the flames subside. Transfer to individual plates, placing 2 crêpes on each plate. Repeat the process in 2 more batches. Serve at once, garnished with the orange zest strips, if desired.

Red Wine–Poached Pears

4 pears, such as Bosc or Anjou, peeled, with stem intact

2½ cups (20 fl oz/625 ml) Pinot Noir or other fruity red wine

½ cup (4 oz/125 g) sugar

1 wide lemon zest strip, 2 inches (5 cm) long

2-inch (5-cm) piece vanilla bean, halved lengthwise

1½ cups (6 oz/185 g) fresh raspberries

MAKES 4 SERVINGS

1 Place the pears in a nonreactive saucepan large enough to hold them lying down. Add 1½ cups (12 fl oz/375 ml) water, the wine, sugar, lemon zest, and vanilla bean. In a food processor or blender, purée 1 cup (4 oz/125 g) of the raspberries until smooth. Pass the purée through a fine-mesh sieve held over the pan holding the pears, pressing with the back of a spoon to push as much of the purée through the sieve as possible. Discard the contents of the sieve.

2 Place the pan over medium-high heat and bring to a boil. Reduce the heat to medium-low, carefully set a heatproof plate on top of the pears to keep them submerged in the liquid, and simmer gently until a thin knife inserted into the widest part of a pear pierces easily to the center, 35–40 minutes. Remove the plate covering the pears. Let the pears cool to room temperature in the liquid.

3 Using a slotted spoon, transfer the pears to shallow individual bowls, or place all 4 pears on a deep platter. Bring the cooking liquid to a boil over high heat and boil until it is reduced by half, about 10 minutes. Pour the liquid over the pears and let the pears cool in the liquid. Remove the zest strip and vanilla bean and discard. Sprinkle the remaining raspberries evenly around the pears, and serve at room temperature.

Crème Brûlée

4 egg yolks

½ tsp pure vanilla extract

2 cups (16 fl oz/500 ml) heavy cream

¼ cup (2 oz/60 g) granulated sugar

Boiling water

2 tbsp firmly packed dark brown sugar

MAKES 4 SERVINGS

1 Preheat the oven to 325°F (165°C). Have ready four ¾-cup (6–fl oz/180-ml) ramekins and a shallow baking pan just large enough to hold them.

2 In a bowl, beat the egg yolks and vanilla until the mixture thickens. Set aside. In a saucepan over medium-high heat, warm the cream and granulated sugar, stirring, until small bubbles form along the edges of the pan and the sugar dissolves, 3–4 minutes. Gradually whisk the cream mixture into the egg yolk mixture. Strain through a fine-mesh sieve into a glass measuring pitcher.

3 Pour the mixture into the ramekins, filling each to ½ inch (12 mm) below the rim. Place the ramekins in the baking dish and pour boiling water into the dish until it reaches halfway up the sides of the ramekins. Bake until the custards are set but still jiggle slightly in the middle when the ramekins are shaken, and a thin skin has formed on top, 35–40 minutes.

4 Transfer the baking dish to a wire rack and let the custards cool slightly. Remove the ramekins from the baking dish and let the custards cool to room temperature. Refrigerate until well chilled, 3–4 hours.

5 When ready to serve, preheat the broiler. Sprinkle the tops of the custards evenly with the brown sugar. Return the ramekins to the baking pan and pour cold water around them. Broil until the brown sugar melts and caramelizes, 2–3 minutes. Alternatively, use a small kitchen torch to caramelize the sugar.

6 Transfer to a wire rack and let the custards cool until the surface hardens, about 10 minutes. Serve at once.

The flavor of this ethereal dessert relies upon the chocolate, so use the best-quality bittersweet chocolate that you can find.

Chocolate Soufflés

Butter for greasing

8 oz (250 g) bittersweet chocolate, chopped

1 cup (8 fl oz/250 ml) heavy cream

1 cup (8 fl oz/250 ml) whole milk

4 eggs, separated and at room temperature, plus 3 egg whites, at room temperature

¼ tsp cream of tartar

¼ cup (2 oz/60 g) granulated sugar

Powdered sugar for garnish

MAKES 6 SERVINGS

1 Preheat the oven to 375°F (190°C). Butter six ¾-cup (6–fl oz/180-ml) soufflé molds or ramekins and place on a baking sheet. Set aside.

2 In a saucepan over medium-low heat, combine the chocolate, cream, and milk and bring to a simmer, whisking until the chocolate melts. Remove from the heat and whisk in the 4 egg yolks.

3 In a bowl, whisk together the 7 egg whites and the cream of tartar until soft peaks form. Add the granulated sugar and whisk until stiff peaks form.

4 Using a rubber spatula, gently fold one-fourth of the egg whites into the chocolate mixture, then fold the chocolate mixture gently into the egg whites.

5 Pour the batter into the prepared soufflé molds, dividing it evenly. Bake until each of the soufflés have risen 2–3 inches (5–7.5 cm) and the centers are still creamy, 20–25 minutes. If desired, continue to bake until a toothpick inserted in the middle comes out clean, 3–5 minutes longer.

6 Put the powdered sugar into a fine-mesh sieve and tap it over the soufflés to dust them with the sugar. Serve at once.

Italian

Imported Italian cannellini beans and good-quality olive oil will deliver authentic flavor in this simple and delicious starter.

White Bean & Arugula Crostini

3 tbsp olive oil, plus extra as needed

2 tbsp finely chopped yellow onion

2 tbsp finely chopped carrot

2 tbsp finely chopped celery

2 cups (14 oz/440 g) cooked cannellini or other white beans, homemade (page 287) or rinsed jarred

Salt and freshly ground pepper

1 baguette

2 cups (2 oz/60 g) baby arugula leaves

MAKES 6–8 SERVINGS

1 Preheat the oven to 375°F (190°C). In a frying pan over medium heat, warm the 3 tbsp olive oil. Add the onion, carrot, and celery and sauté until the onion is golden and the carrot and celery have softened, 5–6 minutes. Add the beans, season with salt and pepper, and stir well to combine. Remove from the heat and let cool to room temperature.

2 Meanwhile, cut the baguette on the diagonal into 18 slices about ½ inch (12 mm) thick each. (You may not need the whole loaf.) Arrange the bread slices on a rimmed baking sheet and brush the tops lightly with olive oil. Bake until golden, about 5 minutes. Remove from the oven.

3 Arrange the toasts on a serving platter or divide among individual plates. Spoon the beans on the toasts, dividing them evenly. Top with the arugula, then drizzle generously with olive oil. Serve at once.

Here is a quick and easy antipasto made with just a few ingredients. Enjoy these flavorful bites with a glass of Prosecco.

Spicy Fried Chickpeas

1 can (15 oz/470 g) chickpeas

Olive or canola oil for frying

3 cloves garlic, unpeeled

6 fresh sage leaves

Salt

Cayenne pepper

MAKES 4–6 SERVINGS

1 Drain the chickpeas in a colander, rinse well with cold water, and then transfer to paper towels and dry thoroughly.

2 Pour oil to a depth of 1 inch (2.5 cm) in a deep, heavy frying pan and heat to 375°F (190°C) on a deep-frying thermometer. Line a rimmed baking sheet with paper towels and set it next to the stove.

3 When the oil is ready, add the garlic cloves and fry until they begin to turn golden, about 1 minute. Add the chickpeas and sage and fry until crisp and browned, 4–5 minutes. Take care when adding the chickpeas as they might spit and sputter due to moisture. Cook them in batches if necessary, allowing the oil to return to 375°F (190°C) before adding the next batch. Using a slotted spoon, transfer the chickpeas, garlic, and sage to the towel-lined baking sheet to drain.

4 Sprinkle the chickpeas with salt and cayenne pepper to taste, transfer to a serving bowl, and serve at once.

Fennel, Orange
& Olive Salad

2 small fennel bulbs

2 blood oranges or
regular oranges

2 tbsp olive oil

Salt and ground white pepper

About 24 Gaeta or other
black olives, pitted

MAKES 4 SERVINGS

1 Cut off the stems and feathery leaves from the fennel bulbs and discard. Cut away and discard any discolored areas of the bulbs. Halve each bulb lengthwise and cut away the tough core, then cut the halves crosswise into very thin slices.

2 Using a sharp knife, cut a slice off both ends of each orange to reveal the flesh. Place the orange upright on the cutting board and, using the knife, cut downward to remove the peel and pith, following the contour of the fruit. Cut the orange in half through the stem end, then slice each half crosswise as thinly as possible. Remove and discard any seeds and visible pith.

3 Divide the fennel slices among 4 plates. Sprinkle the orange slices over the fennel, again dividing evenly, and drizzle the olive oil evenly over the top. Season with salt and white pepper, and scatter about 6 olives on each plate. Let stand for a few minutes before serving.

Tangy blood oranges and briny olives bring emphatic flavor to crisp raw fennel in this winter salad.

Tomato, Basil & Mozzarella Salad

3 or 4 large, ripe tomatoes

½ lb (250 g) fresh
mozzarella cheese

Salt and freshly ground pepper

¼ cup (2 fl oz/60 ml) olive oil

About 10 fresh basil leaves

MAKES 4 SERVINGS

1 Cut the tomatoes and mozzarella into slices about ¼ inch (6 mm) thick.

2 On a serving platter, overlap slices of the tomato and mozzarella. Sprinkle with salt and pepper. Drizzle with the olive oil. Tear the basil into small pieces and sprinkle over the salad. Serve at once.

NOTE For this recipe, it is essential to use the best-quality ripe, fresh tomatoes that you can find. Try different heirloom varieties such as Green Zebra or Brandywine. Visit a well-stocked supermarket or cheese shop for good-quality fresh mozzarella, often sold in small tubs of whey.

For this simple, classic summer salad, southern Italian cooks rely on the very best seasonal ingredients.

These addictive rice croquettes, called *arancini* ("little oranges") in Italian, are stuffed with cheese and prosciutto.

Fried Risotto Balls

2½ cups (20 fl oz/625 ml) chicken stock, homemade (page 283) or purchased

1 cup (7 oz/220 g) Arborio rice

1 tbsp unsalted butter

Salt

½ cup (2 oz/60 g) freshly grated Parmesan cheese

1 whole egg, plus 1 egg yolk

1 cup (5 oz/155 g) flour

2 cups (8 oz/250 g) fine dried bread crumbs

2 oz (60 g) prosciutto, chopped

2 oz (60 g) fresh mozzarella cheese, chopped

3 egg whites, lightly beaten

Canola oil for deep-frying

MAKES 4–6 SERVINGS

1 In a saucepan over high heat, bring the stock to a boil. Stir in the rice, butter, and a pinch of salt. Cover, reduce the heat to low, and cook until the liquid is absorbed and the rice is tender, 18–20 minutes. Transfer the rice to a bowl and stir in the Parmesan. Let cool slightly, then stir in the egg and egg yolk. Set aside to cool completely.

2 Spread the flour and bread crumbs on separate plates. On another plate, mix together the prosciutto and mozzarella, then divide into 12 equal portions. Put the egg whites in a shallow bowl. Moisten your hands with water. Scoop up ¼ cup (1¾ oz/50 g) of the rice mixture and flatten out the mixture in the cupped palm of one hand. Place 1 portion of the prosciutto-mozzarella mixture in the center and mold the rice over the filling. Shape the rice into a ball and roll in the flour, the egg whites and, finally, the bread crumbs. Place on a rack. Continue to make 12 balls total. Let the balls dry for at least 15 minutes, or refrigerate for up to 1 hour.

3 Preheat the oven to 200°F (95°C). Line a large platter with paper towels. Pour oil to a depth of 3 inches (7.5 cm) into a deep, heavy frying pan and heat to 375°F (190°C) on a deep-frying thermometer. Using a slotted spoon, gently lower a few of the rice balls into the hot oil, being careful not to crowd the pan. Fry until golden brown and crisp, 2–3 minutes. Transfer the balls to the platter to drain and place in the oven to keep warm. Fry the remaining balls in the same way. Arrange the risotto balls on a platter and serve at once.

In this cool-weather salad, warm, creamy beans contrast with crisp, slightly bitter radicchio in a bright citrus dressing.

Warm Bean & Radicchio Salad

2 oz (60 g) pancetta, chopped

3 tbsp olive oil

1 clove garlic, lightly crushed

1 sprig fresh rosemary

2 cups (14 oz/440 g) cooked cranberry or cannellini beans, homemade (page 287) or rinsed canned

Salt and freshly ground pepper

1 small head radicchio, trimmed and cut crosswise into narrow strips

1 tbsp fresh lemon juice

2 tbsp minced fresh flat-leaf parsley

MAKES 4 SERVINGS

1 In a large saucepan over medium heat, cook the pancetta, stirring often, until crisp, about 5 minutes. Using a slotted spoon, transfer the pancetta to paper towels to drain.

2 Add 1 tbsp of the olive oil to the fat in the pan and warm over medium heat. Add the garlic and rosemary and sauté until the garlic is lightly golden, about 2 minutes. Stir in the beans and season with salt and pepper. Reduce the heat to medium-low, cover, and simmer, stirring occasionally, for about 5 minutes to blend the flavors.

3 Remove the beans from the heat and remove and discard the rosemary and garlic. In a serving bowl, toss together the beans, radicchio, and reserved pancetta. Add the remaining 2 tbsp oil and the lemon juice and toss again.

4 Taste and adjust the seasoning with salt and pepper, sprinkle with the parsley, and serve at once.

This recipe is inspired by the rustic Italian soup called *pasta e fagioli,* the ingredients for which might already be in your pantry.

Rustic Pasta & Bean Soup

3 tbsp olive oil

1 yellow onion, finely chopped

1 carrot, finely chopped

1 rib celery, thinly sliced

1 large tomato, peeled, seeded (page 290), and finely chopped, or 1 can (14½ oz/455 g) diced tomatoes

8 cups (64 fl oz/2 l) beef or chicken stock, homemade (page 283) or purchased

2 cups (14 oz/440 g) cooked cranberry or cannellini beans, homemade (page 287) or rinsed canned

2 cups (7 oz/220 g) ditalini, tubetti, or other small hollow pasta

Salt and freshly ground pepper

MAKES 6 SERVINGS

1 In a large saucepan over medium heat, warm the olive oil. Add the onion, carrot, and celery and sauté until the onion is golden, 6–8 minutes.

2 Add the tomato, stock, and cooked beans to the pan and bring to a boil. Reduce the heat to medium-low and simmer, stirring occasionally, until the vegetables are tender, about 10 minutes. If desired, to thicken the soup, remove a cupful and purée in a food processor or blender. Add the puréed soup back to the saucepan and stir to combine.

3 Raise the heat to medium, add the pasta, and cook until al dente, about 8 minutes. Season the soup to taste with salt and pepper. Ladle into warmed soup bowls and serve at once.

NOTE In late summer and early autumn you can substitute fresh cranberry beans for the cooked dried beans here. Boil them for about 30 minutes until tender, before adding them to the soup.

Ricotta & Spinach
Gnocchi

8 tbsp (4 oz/125 g)
unsalted butter

1 small yellow onion,
finely chopped

2 cups (16 oz/500 g) whole-milk
ricotta cheese

1¾ cups (7 oz/220 g) freshly
grated Parmesan cheese

2 eggs

¼ tsp freshly grated nutmeg

Salt and freshly ground pepper

2 lb (1 kg) spinach, cooked and
finely chopped (page 287)

1½ cups (7½ oz/235 g) flour

½ cup (2 oz/60 g) fine
dried bread crumbs

MAKES 6 SERVINGS

1 Melt 2 tbsp of the butter in a small frying pan over medium heat. Add the onion and sauté until tender and lightly golden, about 10 minutes. Set aside.

2 In a large bowl, beat together the ricotta, 1 cup (4 oz/125 g) of the Parmesan, the eggs, and the nutmeg. Season with salt and pepper. Add the onion and cooked spinach and stir well. Stir in the flour until well blended.

3 Bring a pot three-fourths full of salted water to a rolling boil. Preheat the oven to 400°F (200°C). Butter a shallow 3-qt (3-l) baking dish with 2 tbsp of the butter. Line 2 rimmed baking sheets with parchment paper. Scoop up tablespoonfuls of the ricotta mixture and, with dampened hands, shape them into ¾-inch (2-cm) balls. Place on the baking sheets without touching.

4 Reduce the heat so the water simmers. In batches without crowding, add the gnocchi to the pot and cook, stirring gently once or twice, until they rise to the surface, about 3 minutes. Using a slotted spoon, transfer them to the prepared baking dish.

5 Cut the remaining 4 tbsp (2 oz/60 g) butter into bits and dot the surface of the gnocchi evenly. Sprinkle with the remaining Parmesan and the bread crumbs. Bake the gnocchi until the butter is sizzling and the cheese is melted, about 15 minutes. Serve at once.

Eggplant &
Ricotta Rolls

1 large eggplant, about 1½ lb
(750 g), trimmed

Salt and freshly ground pepper

1 cup (8 oz/250 g) whole-milk
ricotta cheese

¼ lb (125 g) fresh mozzarella
cheese, shredded

4 tbsp (1 oz/30 g) freshly grated
Parmesan cheese

1 tbsp minced fresh
flat-leaf parsley

Olive oil for brushing

2½ cups (20 fl oz/625 ml)
Classic Tomato Sauce
(page 284)

MAKES 4 SERVINGS

1 Cut the eggplant crosswise on the diagonal into slices about ¼ inch (6 mm) thick. Layer the slices in a colander set over a plate, sprinkling each layer with salt, and let stand for 30 minutes to drain.

2 Preheat the oven to 450°F (230°C). In a bowl, stir together the ricotta, mozzarella, 2 tbsp of the Parmesan, the parsley, and pepper to taste.

3 Rinse the eggplant slices under cold water and pat dry with paper towels. Brush the slices on both sides with olive oil and arrange them in a single layer on a rimmed baking sheet.

4 Bake the eggplant slices until lightly golden brown on the bottom, about 10 minutes. Turn the slices over and continue to bake until browned on the other side, 5–10 minutes longer. Remove the eggplant from the oven. Reduce the oven temperature to 350°F (180°C).

5 Spoon a thin layer of the tomato sauce into a 9-inch (23-cm) square baking dish. To make each eggplant roll, place a spoonful of the cheese mixture near one end of a slice and roll up the slice. As each roll is formed, place it seam side down in the dish. Spoon the remaining sauce over the rolls, then sprinkle evenly with the remaining 2 tbsp Parmesan.

6 Bake until the sauce is bubbling hot and the rolls are heated through, about 25 minutes. Divide the rolls among individual plates and serve at once.

This pretty risotto showcases delicately flavored sweet peas and earthy asparagus, two early harbingers of spring.

Risotto with Spring Vegetables

Salt and freshly ground pepper

1 lb (500 g) slender asparagus, trimmed and cut into 2-inch (5-cm) lengths

7–8 cups (56–64 fl oz/1.75–2 l) chicken stock, homemade (page 283) or purchased

¼ cup (2 fl oz/60 ml) olive oil

1 leek, white and tender green part, sliced crosswise

3 cups (21 oz/655 g) Arborio rice

1 cup (8 fl oz/250 ml) dry white wine

1 cup (5 oz/155 g) fresh or thawed frozen peas

1 tbsp unsalted butter

¼ cup (1 oz/30 g) freshly grated Parmesan cheese

MAKES 6 SERVINGS

1 Bring a large saucepan three-fourths full of salted water to a boil. Add the asparagus and cook until nearly tender, 1–2 minutes. Drain and rinse under running cold water. Set aside. Add the stock to the saucepan and bring to a simmer over medium heat. Reduce heat to low to keep warm.

2 In a deep, heavy saucepan over medium-high heat, warm the olive oil. Add the leek and sauté until softened, 2–3 minutes. Stir in the rice and reduce the heat to medium. Cook, stirring, until the rice grains are evenly coated with the oil and the grains turn translucent at the edges, about 3 minutes. Pour in the wine and stir until it is completely absorbed. Add the warm stock a ladleful at a time, stirring frequently after each addition. Wait until the stock is almost completely absorbed before adding the next ladleful. Reserve ¼ cup (2 fl oz/60 ml) stock to add at the end.

3 When the rice looks creamy and is almost tender to the bite, after about 20 minutes, add the asparagus, peas, and a ladleful of stock. Cook, stirring occasionally, until the vegetables are heated through and just tender, about 3 minutes longer. You may find that you did not need all of the stock or that you need more. If more liquid is required, use hot water.

4 Remove the risotto from the heat and stir in the butter, Parmesan cheese, and the reserved ¼ cup stock. Season to taste with salt and pepper. Spoon into warmed bowls and serve at once.

Puttanesca, or "harlot-style," is a tongue-in-cheek Italian name for the spicy and salty tomato-based sauce served here over penne.

Pasta with Spicy Tomato-Olive Sauce

¼ cup (2 fl oz/60 ml) olive oil

2 cloves garlic, minced

½ tsp red pepper flakes

1 can (28 oz/875 g) diced tomatoes, drained

Salt and freshly ground black pepper

6–8 olive oil–packed anchovy fillets, chopped

¼ cup (1½ oz/45 g) pitted Gaeta or other Mediterranean-style black olives

2 tbsp chopped rinsed capers

2 tbsp minced fresh flat-leaf parsley

1 lb (500 g) penne or other tubular pasta

MAKES 4–6 SERVINGS

1 In a large frying pan over medium heat, warm the oil. Add the garlic and red pepper flakes and sauté until the garlic is lightly golden, about 2 minutes. Add the tomatoes, 1 tsp salt, and a pinch of black pepper and bring to a simmer. Reduce the heat to low and cook uncovered, stirring occasionally, until thickened, about 20 minutes. Add the anchovies, olives, capers, and parsley and simmer for 1 minute longer. Taste and adjust the seasoning.

2 While the sauce simmers, bring a large pot three-fourths full of salted water to a rolling boil. Add the penne and cook, stirring occasionally, until al dente, according to the package directions. Scoop out and reserve about 2 ladlefuls of the cooking water, then drain the pasta.

3 Add the drained pasta to the sauce in the pan and stir and toss over low heat until well coated, adjusting the consistency with some of the cooking water if needed. Transfer to a warmed serving bowl and serve at once.

The pleasantly bitter flavor of broccoli rabe makes an appealing contrast to the sweet pork sausage in this sauce.

Orecchiette with Sausage

⅓ cup (3 fl oz/80 ml) plus 1 tbsp olive oil

½ cup (2 oz/60 g) fine dried bread crumbs

Salt

1½ lb (750 g) broccoli rabe, trimmed

1 lb (500 g) orecchiette, conchigliette, or other shell pasta

½ lb (250 g) sweet Italian sausages, casings discarded and meat coarsely chopped

4 large cloves garlic, minced

Pinch of red pepper flakes

½ cup (2 oz/60 g) freshly grated *pecorino romano* or Parmesan cheese

MAKES 4–6 SERVINGS

1 In a frying pan over medium-low heat, warm the 1 tbsp olive oil. Add the bread crumbs and stir to coat them with the oil. Season lightly with salt and cook, stirring often, until the crumbs are an even, deep golden brown, about 10 minutes. Pour onto a plate and set aside to cool.

2 Bring a large pot three-fourths full of salted water to a rolling boil. Add the broccoli rabe and cook, testing often, until the stems are just tender, 2–3 minutes. Using tongs or a wire-mesh skimmer, lift out the broccoli rabe into a sieve and cool it quickly under running cold water. Drain and squeeze gently to remove excess moisture. Chop coarsely and set aside.

3 Add the orecchiette to the boiling water and cook, stirring occasionally, until al dente, according to the package directions.

4 Meanwhile, warm the ⅓ cup olive oil in the frying pan over medium-low heat. Add the sausage, garlic, and red pepper flakes and cook, stirring and breaking up the sausage meat with a wooden spoon, until the sausage is browned, about 7 minutes. Add the broccoli rabe and stir to combine with the sausage. Cook until the broccoli rabe is heated through, about 2 minutes. Season to taste with salt.

5 When the orecchiette is ready, scoop out and reserve about 2 ladlefuls of the cooking water, then drain the pasta and return it to the pot. Add the sausage mixture and the cheese to the pot and stir over low heat to combine, adjusting the consistency with some of the cooking water if needed.

6 Divide among warmed plates, top each portion with a sprinkle of toasted bread crumbs, and serve at once. Pass the remaining crumbs at the table.

Serve this Genoese-style dish for lunch in early summer, when slender green beans, new potatoes, and basil are all plentiful.

Penne with Pesto & Green Beans

Salt

½ lb (250 g) small red potatoes, peeled and sliced

½ lb (250 g) young, slender green beans, stem ends trimmed

1 lb (500 g) penne or ziti pasta

½ cup (4 fl oz/125 ml) pesto, homemade (page 285) or purchased

1 tbsp unsalted butter, at room temperature

MAKES 4–6 SERVINGS

1 Bring a large pot three-fourths full of salted water to a rolling boil. Add the potatoes and cook until tender-crisp, about 5 minutes. Add the green beans to the potatoes and continue to cook until the potatoes and beans are tender, about 5 minutes more. Using a large slotted spoon, transfer the potatoes and beans to a large warmed serving bowl. Cover the bowl loosely with aluminum foil to keep the vegetables warm.

2 Bring the water back to a rolling boil, add the penne, and cook, stirring occasionally, until al dente, according to the package directions. Scoop out and reserve about 2 ladlefuls of the cooking water, then drain the pasta.

3 Add the drained pasta to the bowl with the vegetables and then add the pesto. Stir and toss until the pasta and vegetables are well coated, adjusting the consistency with some of the cooking water if needed. Add the butter and toss to coat evenly. Serve at once.

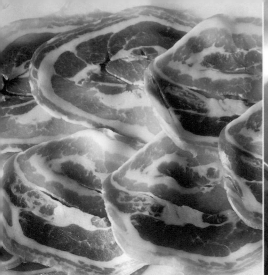

Spaghetti alla Carbonara

6 oz (185 g) pancetta
or bacon, chopped

1 tbsp olive oil

Salt and freshly ground pepper

1 lb (500 g) spaghetti

¼ cup (1 oz/30 g) freshly grated
pecorino romano cheese

¼ cup (1 oz/30 g) freshly grated
Parmesan cheese

2 eggs plus 1 egg yolk,
at room temperature

MAKES 4–6 SERVINGS

1 In a large frying pan over medium-low heat, combine the pancetta and olive oil and heat slowly until much of the fat is rendered and the pancetta has browned a little, about 15 minutes. Remove from the heat, leave the pancetta and fat in the pan, and cover to keep warm.

2 Bring a large pot three-fourths full of salted water to a rolling boil. Add the spaghetti, stir well, and cook, stirring occasionally, until al dente, according to the package directions.

3 While the spaghetti is cooking, in a bowl, mix together the cheeses. In another bowl, whisk together the eggs and egg yolk until well blended. Stir the cheese mixture and several grinds of pepper into the eggs.

4 From this point on, timing and temperature are crucial. Put a large serving bowl in the sink and set a colander in the serving bowl. When the spaghetti is ready, pour it into the colander, so that its cooking water will warm the serving bowl. Grab the colander quickly out of the water and shake a couple of times. Toss the drained spaghetti into the pan with the pancetta and stir a couple of times to coat the pasta with the fat. Being careful not to burn your fingers, empty the hot water from the serving bowl, reserving a cupful. Transfer the pasta to the warmed bowl, add the egg mixture, and stir and toss vigorously with a wooden spoon to coat the pasta evenly. Adjust the consistency of the sauce with some of the cooking water if needed. Divide among warmed plates or shallow bowls and serve at once.

Spinach-Ricotta Lasagna

4 cups (2 lb/1 kg)
ricotta cheese

½ cup (2 oz/60 g) freshly grated
Parmesan cheese

1½ cups (6 oz/185 g) shredded
fresh mozzarella cheese

2 eggs, lightly beaten

2 cloves garlic, minced

Salt and freshly ground pepper

6 cups (48 fl oz/1.5 l) Classic
Tomato Sauce (page 284)

9 no-boil lasagna noodles

3 large red bell peppers,
roasted (page 291),
seeded, and chopped

4 lb (2 kg) fresh spinach, cooked
and chopped (page 287), or
2 lb (1 kg) frozen chopped
spinach, cooked

MAKES 8–10 SERVINGS

1 Preheat the oven to 350°F (180°C). In a large bowl, combine the ricotta, Parmesan, ½ cup (2 oz/60 g) of the mozzarella, eggs, garlic, 1 tsp salt, and ¼ tsp pepper and stir until well combined.

2 To assemble the lasagna, in the bottom of a 9-by-13-by-3-inch (23-by-33-by-7.5 cm) baking dish, spread about 2 cups (16 fl oz/500 ml) of the tomato sauce in an even layer. Arrange 3 of the lasagna noodles on top of the sauce. Cover the noodles evenly with half of the bell peppers. Cover the peppers with half of the spinach, using your fingers to pull any clumps apart. Using a large spoon, dollop half of the cheese mixture on top of the spinach. With the back of the spoon, gently spread the cheese as much as possible without pulling up the spinach. Top with 1 cup (8 fl oz/250 ml) of the tomato sauce. Add another layer of the pasta, then the remaining peppers, spinach, and cheese mixture, and then 1 cup of the tomato sauce. Cover with the remaining 3 lasagna noodles. Spread the remaining 2 cups tomato sauce over the top. Cover the baking dish with aluminum foil.

3 Bake until the pasta is almost soft when tested with a knife, about 1 hour. Uncover the lasagna. Sprinkle the remaining 1 cup (4 oz/125 g) mozzarella evenly over the top. Replace the foil. Continue to bake until the pasta is soft and the cheese on top of the lasagna is melted, about 15 minutes longer. Remove from the oven, uncover and let the lasagna rest for 20 minutes. Cut into squares and serve at once.

Here, *salsa verde*, a flavorful Italian-style green sauce, gilds tender grilled halibut, but it's also excellent with tuna or swordfish.

Halibut with Salsa Verde

2 cups (2 oz/60 g) fresh flat-leaf parsley leaves

1 clove garlic

¼ cup (½ oz/15 g) crustless coarse country bread cubes

4 olive oil–packed anchovy fillets

2 tbsp capers, rinsed

⅔ cup (5 fl oz/160 ml) plus 2 tbsp olive oil

1–2 tbsp fresh lemon juice

Salt and freshly ground pepper

4 halibut fillets, each about 1 inch (2.5 cm) thick

Lemon wedges for serving

MAKES 4 SERVINGS

1 In a food processor, process the parsley, garlic, bread cubes, anchovies, and capers until finely chopped. With the motor running, slowly drizzle in the ⅔ cup olive oil in a thin, steady stream and process until a smooth, flowing sauce forms. Transfer to a bowl, add the lemon juice and salt to taste, and let stand at room temperature for 1 hour.

2 Rub the fish fillets on both sides with the 2 tbsp olive oil, and then season both sides with salt and pepper.

3 Prepare a gas or charcoal grill for direct grilling over medium-high heat (page 293). Oil the grill rack. Place the fish directly over the heat elements or over the hottest part of the fire. Cook the fish, turning once, until opaque throughout when tested with a knife, 5–7 minutes on each side. Alternatively, preheat a stove-top grill pan over medium-high heat and brush generously with oil. Cook as directed for the grill.

4 Transfer the fish to warmed plates and serve at once, accompanied with the sauce and lemon wedges.

In Italy, grilled fish is treated simply, often with nothing more than olive oil and salt and perhaps some lemon and rosemary.

Swordfish with Rosemary & Lemon

6–8 lemons

4 tbsp (2 fl oz/60 ml) olive oil, plus extra as needed

Salt and freshly ground pepper

2 cloves garlic, minced

3 tbsp minced fresh rosemary

4 swordfish or mahimahi fillets, each about 6 oz (185 g) and 1 inch (2.5 cm) thick

MAKES 4 SERVINGS

1 Juice enough of the lemons to yield ⅓ cup (3 fl oz/80 ml) juice. Thinly slice the remaining lemons into rounds about ⅛ inch (3 mm) thick, discarding the ends. Arrange the lemon slices on a plate in a single layer. Drizzle with 1 tbsp of the olive oil and sprinkle with salt and pepper. Set aside.

2 In a shallow dish, whisk together the lemon juice, the remaining 3 tbsp olive oil, the garlic, and the rosemary. Season the fish generously with salt and pepper, then place in the marinade and turn to coat. Cover and refrigerate for about 30 minutes.

3 Prepare a gas or charcoal grill for direct grilling over medium-high heat (page 293). Oil the grill rack.

4 Using a slotted spatula or spoon, lift the fish from the marinade and arrange directly over the heat elements or over the hottest part of the fire. Discard the marinade. Grill the fish, turning once, until opaque throughout but still moist looking in the center when tested with a knife, 8–9 minutes total. Grill the lemon slices alongside the fish, turning them once, until they are browned and soft, 1–2 minutes on each side.

5 Transfer the fish to a warm platter or individual plates and arrange 2 or more lemon slices over each piece. Serve at once.

Balsamic Braised Chicken

1 chicken, about 3 lb (1.5 kg),
cut into 8 serving pieces
(page 293)

Salt and freshly ground pepper

2 tbsp olive oil

2 cloves garlic, unpeeled

1 sprig fresh rosemary

1 cup (8 fl oz/250 ml) Chianti
or other dry red wine

¼ cup (2 fl oz/60 ml)
balsamic vinegar

MAKES 4 SERVINGS

1 Pat the chicken pieces dry with paper towels and sprinkle with salt and pepper. In a large frying pan over medium-high heat, warm the olive oil. Add the chicken and garlic and cook the chicken, turning as needed, until well browned on both sides, about 20 minutes total. Adjust the heat as needed to prevent the garlic from burning.

2 Tip the pan and spoon off the excess fat. Add the rosemary sprig, wine, and vinegar and bring to a simmer. Reduce the heat to medium, cover, and cook, turning the chicken pieces occasionally, until the chicken is opaque throughout when tested with a knife, about 15 minutes. Transfer the chicken pieces to a warmed platter, cover, and keep warm.

3 Raise the heat to high, bring the liquid to a boil, and cook until the liquid is reduced and thickened, creating a flavorful pan sauce. Remove and discard the garlic cloves and the rosemary sprig. Taste and adjust the seasoning with salt and pepper. Spoon the sauce over the chicken and serve at once.

Both balsamic vinegar and Chianti hail from northern Italy. Together, they give the chicken a beautiful mahogany color.

Chicken Saltimbocca

4 skinless, boneless chicken breast halves

4 large slices Fontina or Jarlsberg cheese

4 slices prosciutto, trimmed of all visible fat

¼ cup (1½ oz/45 g) flour

¾ cup (3 oz/90 g) Italian-seasoned fine dried bread crumbs

1 egg white

1 tbsp whole milk

3 tsp olive oil

MAKES 4 SERVINGS

1 Cut each chicken breast in half crosswise so you have a total of 8 pieces. Working with 1 piece of chicken at a time, place it between 2 sheets of waxed paper or plastic wrap and, using a meat pounder, pound to flatten to an even thickness of ½ inch (12 mm).

2 Place 1 slice of cheese on 1 of the chicken pieces. Trim the cheese to fit. Place 1 prosciutto slice on top of the cheese, folding it so it fits neatly. Top with a second piece of chicken. Repeat to make 4 stuffed breasts in all.

3 Preheat the oven to 350°F (180°C). Spread the flour and bread crumbs on separate plates. In a bowl, beat the egg white with the milk until blended. Dredge each stuffed breast in flour, shaking off the excess. Turn it in the egg white mixture and then dredge it in the bread crumbs, coating it evenly and pressing the crumbs in with your fingers. Set each breaded breast on a plate.

4 In an ovenproof frying pan over medium-high heat, warm half of the olive oil. Add the stuffed breasts and cook until browned on the bottom, about 4 minutes. Drizzle the remaining 1½ tsp oil in the pan around the chicken, carefully turn the breasts, and brown on the other side, 3–4 minutes longer. Place the pan in the oven and bake until the chicken is opaque throughout when tested with a knife, 15–17 minutes. Serve at once.

Sweet sautéed peppers and salty black olives brighten succulent braised pork chops in this southern Italian-style dish.

Pork Chops with Peppers

4 center-cut pork loin chops, each about 1 inch (2.5 cm) thick, trimmed of excess fat

Salt and freshly ground pepper

2 tbsp olive oil

1 large yellow onion, halved and thinly sliced

3 red bell peppers, seeded and cut into strips

1 large green bell pepper, seeded and cut into strips

1 large yellow bell pepper, seeded and cut into strips

1 tbsp chopped fresh oregano

2 tbsp red wine vinegar

¼ cup (1½ oz/45 g) oil-cured black olives, pitted

MAKES 4 SERVINGS

1 Pat the pork chops dry with paper towels. Sprinkle with salt and pepper. In a large frying pan over medium-high heat, warm 1 tbsp of the olive oil. Add the pork chops and cook, turning once, until browned on both sides, about 5 minutes on each side. Transfer the chops to a plate and cover loosely with aluminum foil to keep warm.

2 Add the remaining 1 tbsp olive oil to the pan. Add the onion and cook, stirring often, until translucent, about 4 minutes. Add the red, green, and yellow bell peppers, season to taste with salt and pepper, and cook, stirring often, until the peppers are tender, about 5 minutes. Add the oregano and vinegar. Return the chops to the pan, along with any accumulated juices, and cover them with the onion and peppers. Cover the pan, reduce the heat to medium-low, and simmer until the peppers are soft and the chops are tender but still pale pink and juicy when cut into the center with a knife, about 15 minutes. Stir the olives into the pepper mixture.

3 Transfer the chops to a warmed platter or individual plates, spoon the olives, onion, and peppers over the top, and serve at once.

This simply prepared steak is large enough to serve two. Traditionally, the meat is well browned on the outside and rare inside.

Florentine Steak

1 T-bone or porterhouse steak, cut from the rib with the bone, 1½ lb (750 g)

2 tbsp olive oil, plus extra for drizzling

Salt and freshly ground pepper

Lemon wedges for garnish

1½ cups (1½ oz/45 g) baby arugula for garnish

MAKES 2 SERVINGS

1 Take the meat out of the refrigerator about 1 hour before cooking it to allow it to come to room temperature. Prepare a gas or charcoal grill for direct grilling over medium-high heat (page 293). Oil the grill rack.

2 Rub the meat on both sides with the 2 tbsp olive oil. Using tongs, lay the steak directly over the heat elements or over the hottest part of the fire. Cook until browned on the first side, 5–7 minutes. Turn the steak and sprinkle with salt. Cook on the other side until browned, 5–7 minutes longer. Then turn the meat over once again and sprinkle with salt.

3 Transfer the steak to a cutting board and season generously with pepper. Let the meat rest for 5–10 minutes. Transfer to a platter and garnish with the lemon wedges, arugula, and a drizzle of olive oil. Serve at once.

Meatballs in Tomato-Herb Sauce

2 lb (1 kg) mixed ground beef, pork, and veal

1 egg

1 yellow onion, finely chopped

½ cup (1 oz/30 g) fresh bread crumbs

¼ cup (1 oz/30 g) pine nuts, toasted (page 290)

¼ cup (1½ oz/45 g) freshly grated Parmesan cheese

2 tbsp minced fresh flat-leaf parsley

1 tbsp minced fresh oregano

3 tbsp minced fresh basil

Salt and freshly ground pepper

2 tbsp olive oil

3 cloves garlic, minced

1 can (28 oz/875 g) diced tomatoes in purée

½ cup (4 fl oz/125 ml) dry white wine

MAKES 4 SERVINGS

1 In a large bowl, combine the ground meats, egg, half of the chopped onion, the bread crumbs, pine nuts, Parmesan, parsley, oregano, 1 tbsp of the basil, ¾ tsp salt, and ½ tsp pepper. With dampened hands, gently but thoroughly blend the ingredients. Form the mixture into meatballs about 2 inches (5 cm) in diameter. Set aside.

2 In a small Dutch oven over medium heat, warm the olive oil. Add the remaining onion and sauté until softened, 4–5 minutes. Add the garlic and sauté for 30 seconds. Stir in the diced tomatoes and wine and bring to a boil. Add the meatballs to the sauce, gently spooning the sauce over them. Bring to a simmer, reduce the heat to medium-low, cover, and cook until the meatballs are firm and cooked through, 20–30 minutes.

3 Remove from the heat and let stand for 5 minutes. Stir in the remaining 2 tbsp basil. Divide the meatballs and tomato sauce among warmed plates and serve at once.

Frittata with
Leeks & Herbs

2 tbsp unsalted butter

4 cups (12 oz/375 g) thinly sliced leeks, white and tender green parts only

Salt and freshly ground pepper

6 eggs

½ cup (¾ oz/20 g) mixed minced fresh flat-leaf parsley, basil, and mint

¼ cup (1 oz/30 g) freshly grated Parmesan cheese

MAKES 4 SERVINGS

1 Melt the butter in an ovenproof 10-inch (25-cm) frying pan over medium heat. Add the leeks, season with salt and pepper, and cook, stirring, until softened, about 15 minutes. Reduce the heat as needed to keep the leeks from browning too much.

2 In a bowl, whisk the eggs until well blended. Whisk in the herbs and Parmesan, and season with salt and pepper. Pour the eggs into the pan and stir to distribute the leeks evenly. Reduce the heat to low and cook, using a spatula to lift the edges of the egg to allow the uncooked egg to flow underneath, until the edges and bottom are set but the center is still moist, 13–15 minutes. Preheat the broiler.

3 Place the pan under the broiler about 6 inches (15 cm) from the heat source. Broil until the top is lightly colored and the center is firm, about 1 minute. Using a wide spatula, carefully transfer the frittata to a cutting board. Cut into wedges and serve at once.

Replace the leeks with almost any sautéed vegetable you like, from zucchini to sweet peppers.

Meaty artichokes, gently cooked in a flavorful sauce, make a satisfying accompaniment to roasted pork loin, chicken, or beef.

Braised Artichoke Hearts

2 tbsp olive oil

1 small yellow onion, finely chopped

2 small carrots, sliced

4 large artichokes, trimmed down to the hearts (page 291)

1 cup (8 fl oz/250 ml) chicken stock, homemade (page 283) or purchased

1 tbsp long-grain white rice

½ lemon

Salt and freshly ground pepper

1 tbsp chopped fresh dill

MAKES 4 SERVINGS

1 In a large saucepan over medium-high heat, warm the olive oil. Add the onion and cook, stirring, until translucent, about 4 minutes. Add the carrots and cook, stirring, until softened, about 1 minute longer.

2 Drain the artichoke hearts and pat dry with paper towels. Add them to the saucepan. Stir in the stock and rice. Add ½ cup (4 fl oz/125 ml) water and squeeze in the juice from the lemon half. Season with salt and pepper. When the liquid reaches a boil, reduce the heat to medium-low, cover, and simmer until the artichokes are just tender and the tip of a knife still meets some resistance, about 15 minutes. Uncover and raise the heat to bring the liquid to a boil. Boil until the liquid is reduced and soupy, 8–10 minutes. Transfer the contents of the pan to a serving platter and let stand until the vegetables cool to room temperature.

3 Garnish with the dill and serve at once. Or, cover with plastic wrap and refrigerate for up to 24 hours, then bring to room temperature and add the dill just before serving.

This rich gelato gains a subtle hint of flavor from orange zest. For a special treat, serve it alongside Pistachio Cake (page 99).

Orange-Scented Gelato

2 cups (16 fl oz/500 ml) whole milk

1 cup (8 fl oz/250 ml) heavy cream

Grated zest of 1 orange

6 egg yolks

⅔ cup (5 oz/155 g) sugar

MAKES ABOUT 5 CUPS
(40 FL OZ/1.25 L),
OR 8 SERVINGS

1 In a saucepan over medium heat, combine the milk, cream, and orange zest and heat, stirring occasionally, until small bubbles appear around the edges of the pan. Remove the pan from the heat.

2 In a large bowl, whisk together the egg yolks and sugar until pale and creamy, about 3 minutes. Slowly add the hot milk mixture to the egg mixture while whisking constantly. Return the mixture to the same saucepan and cook over medium-low heat, stirring constantly with a wooden spoon, until the custard has thickened enough to coat the back of the spoon, 5–6 minutes. Do not allow the mixture to come to a simmer. Immediately remove from the heat and pour through a fine-mesh sieve placed over a bowl. Let cool to room temperature, then cover and refrigerate until well chilled, at least 3 hours or up to overnight.

3 Pour the mixture into an ice-cream maker and freeze according to the manufacturer's instructions. The gelato can be served at once while it is still soft, or you can transfer it to a freezer-safe container, cover, and freeze until firm, at least 3 hours or for up to 2 days.

Panna Cotta with Berries

2½ tsp (1 package) unflavored gelatin

¼ cup (2 fl oz/60 ml) whole milk

2 cups (16 fl oz/500 ml) heavy cream

¼ cup (2 oz/60 g) sugar

1 vanilla bean, split in half lengthwise

1 cup (4 oz/125 g) fresh blackberries, raspberries, or other berries, in any combination

MAKES 4 SERVINGS

1 In a large bowl, sprinkle the gelatin over the milk. Let stand for about 2 minutes to soften the gelatin.

2 In a saucepan over medium heat, stir together the cream and sugar. Using the tip of a small, sharp knife, scrape the seeds from the vanilla bean into the cream. Add the vanilla bean pod to the cream. Heat, stirring occasionally, until small bubbles appear around the edges of the pan. Remove from the heat and let cool briefly.

3 Remove the vanilla bean pod. Slowly add the warm cream to the gelatin mixture, stirring constantly until completely dissolved. Pour the mixture into four ¾-cup (6–fl oz/180-ml) ramekins or custard cups, dividing it evenly. Cover and refrigerate for at least 4 hours or up to overnight.

4 When ready to serve, run a small, thin knife around the inside of each ramekin to loosen the *panna cotta,* and then invert each ramekin onto a dessert plate. Arrange the berries alongside and serve at once.

Panna cotta means "cooked cream" in Italian. Here, its ethereal texture is a tempting backdrop for tart berries.

Roasted Strawberries

1 lb (500 g) strawberries, stems removed

2 tbsp aged balsamic vinegar

Freshly ground pepper

2 tbsp unsalted butter

2 tbsp firmly packed golden brown sugar

1 cup (8 oz/250 g) mascarpone, Greek-style yogurt, or vanilla ice cream for serving

MAKES 4 SERVINGS

1 Put the strawberries in a bowl and sprinkle with the vinegar and ½ tsp pepper. Toss to coat evenly. Let stand at room temperature for 20 minutes.

2 Position a rack in the lower third of the oven and preheat the oven to 400°F (200°C). Select a shallow baking dish just large enough to hold the strawberries in a single layer. Put the butter in the dish and place in the preheating oven. Watch carefully to prevent burning. When the butter has melted, remove the dish from the oven and tilt to coat with the butter. Transfer the strawberries and any accumulated juices to the dish. Sprinkle with the sugar and toss gently. Spread out the strawberries in a single layer.

3 Roast the strawberries until they are soft and the liquid is syrupy, about 25 minutes. Remove the dish from the oven and let the berries cool slightly. To serve, divide the mascarpone among individual bowls, spooning the berries and pan juices on top.

The surprising combination of balsamic vinegar and black pepper pairs well with sweet strawberries.

Pistachios and orange zest give this Sicilian cake an intriguing flavor. It is delicious accompanied by a scoop of gelato (page 94).

Pistachio Cake

2 cups (8 oz/250 g) shelled pistachios, lightly toasted (page 290)

1¼ cups (10 oz/315 g) granulated sugar

1 cup (5 oz/155 g) flour

½ tsp grated orange zest

6 egg whites, at room temperature

⅛ tsp salt

1 tsp pure vanilla extract

6 tbsp (3 oz/90 g) unsalted butter, melted and cooled

Powdered sugar for dusting (optional)

MAKES ONE 9-INCH (23-CM) CAKE

1 Preheat the oven to 350°F (180°C). Butter a 9-inch (23-cm) springform pan. Line the bottom with parchment paper cut to fit. Butter the paper.

2 In a food processor, coarsely chop half of the toasted nuts, then remove and set aside. Add the remaining toasted nuts and ½ cup (4 oz/125 g) of the granulated sugar to the food processor and process until the nuts are finely chopped. Add the flour and orange zest and pulse to blend.

3 In a large bowl, using an electric mixer on medium speed, beat together the egg whites and salt until foamy. Increase the speed to high and gradually add the remaining ¾ cup (6 oz/190 g) granulated sugar and the vanilla, beating until soft peaks form.

4 Sprinkle the flour-nut mixture on top of the whites and fold in gently with a rubber spatula. Add the melted butter and reserved chopped nuts and fold in gently. Scrape the batter into the prepared pan.

5 Bake the cake until a toothpick inserted into the center comes out clean, about 40 minutes. Let cool in the pan on a wire rack for about 10 minutes. Run a thin knife around the inside edge of the pan, then remove the pan sides. Using the knife to help loosen it, slide the cake off the parchment and pan bottom and onto the rack. Let the cake cool completely.

6 To serve, place the cake on a serving platter. Using a fine-mesh sieve, dust the top of the cake with powdered sugar, if desired. Serve in wedges.

Mediterranean

This traditional Spanish tapa is a cinch to prepare. Be sure to use very ripe tomatoes so that they dissolve into the toasted bread.

Tomato Bread with Serrano Ham

4 slices coarse country bread, each about ¾ inch (2 cm) thick

1 clove garlic, halved crosswise

Extra-virgin olive oil for brushing

2 ripe, juicy tomatoes

Salt and freshly ground pepper

4 thin slices serrano ham or prosciutto

MAKES 4 SERVINGS

1 Preheat a stove-top grill pan to medium-high, or the oven to 450°F (230°C). Place the bread slices on the grill pan or oven rack and grill or toast, turning once, until crisp and grill-marked on both sides, 3–4 minutes total. Rub one side of each bread slice with the cut side of a piece of garlic. Brush the bread lightly on both sides with olive oil.

2 Arrange the bread slices on a serving platter or individual plates, garlic side up. Cut the tomatoes in half crosswise. Using 1 tomato half for each bread slice, rub the cut side of the tomato vigorously over the bread while squeezing it gently, so that its juices and flesh soak into the bread. Season to taste with salt and pepper. Drape a slice of ham over each slice of bread. Serve at once.

Serve this refreshing Greek spread as a dip with toasted pita or as an accompaniment to grilled lamb kebabs or other meats.

Creamy Cucumber-Yogurt Spread

1 English cucumber

Salt and ground white pepper

1 or 2 cloves garlic

1½ cups (12 oz/375 g) plain Greek-style yogurt

1 tbsp olive oil

1 tbsp fresh lemon juice

1 tbsp red wine vinegar

1 tbsp minced fresh mint

3–4 toasted pita breads, halved, for serving

MAKES 6–8 SERVINGS

1 Peel the cucumber, halve it lengthwise, and then slice it crosswise. Place the cucumber in a colander and sprinkle liberally with salt. Set the colander over a bowl and let drain in the refrigerator for 1 hour. A handful at a time, squeeze the cucumbers to extract any remaining moisture, then spread on paper towels and pat dry. Transfer the cucumbers to a bowl.

2 On a cutting board, sprinkle 1 tsp salt over the garlic. Using a large knife, alternately chop the garlic and press with the side of the blade until it is a lumpy paste, about 3 minutes. Add the garlic paste to the cucumbers and, using a fork, toss to mix. Add the yogurt, olive oil, lemon juice, and vinegar and mix until well combined. Season to taste with white pepper. Transfer to a serving bowl, sprinkle with the mint, and serve at once with the pita.

NOTE For a delicious Middle Eastern meze—perfect for entertaining—serve this spread with an array of purchased olives, roasted peppers, hummus, baba ganoush, tabbouleh (page 118), and toasted pita wedges.

Stuffed Piquillo Peppers

10 oz (315 g) fresh goat cheese, at room temperature

3 tbsp minced fresh chives, plus extra for garnish

3 tbsp minced fresh basil

Salt and freshly ground pepper

1 jar (12 oz/375 g) roasted piquillo peppers

⅓ cup (3 fl oz/80 ml) plus 1 tbsp olive oil

3½ tbsp balsamic vinegar

1 shallot, minced

MAKES 6–8 SERVINGS

1 Preheat the broiler. In a bowl, mash the goat cheese together with the 3 tbsp chives and the basil, then season with salt and pepper to taste.

2 Drain the peppers, but do not rinse them. If necessary, carefully remove the stem, seeds, and ribs from the inside of the peppers without tearing the pepper walls. With a small spoon or your fingers, carefully stuff about 1 tbsp of the goat cheese mixture inside each pepper. The cheese mixture should fill the peppers but should not be bursting out.

3 Arrange the peppers in a single layer on a rimmed baking sheet. Brush them with the 1 tbsp olive oil. Slide the pan under the broiler about 6 inches (15 cm) from the heat source and broil until the cheese is soft and bubbly, about 7 minutes. Let cool slightly.

4 Meanwhile, make a vinaigrette. In a small bowl, whisk together the ⅓ cup olive oil, vinegar, shallot, ¼ tsp salt, and ⅛ tsp pepper.

5 Transfer the peppers to a serving platter. Drizzle liberally with the vinaigrette, sprinkle with extra chives, and serve at once.

Spanish Tortilla

⅓ cup (3 fl oz/80 ml)
olive oil

2 lb (1 kg) waxy potatoes,
peeled and cut into slices about
¼ inch (6 mm) thick

Salt and freshly ground pepper

1 yellow onion, thinly sliced

1 leek, white part only,
thinly sliced crosswise

6 eggs

MAKES 6–8 SERVINGS

1 In a large nonstick frying pan over low heat, warm the olive oil. Add half of the potatoes, season with salt and pepper, and fry, turning occasionally, until the slices are tender but not browned, about 15 minutes. Using a slotted spoon, transfer the potatoes to a colander placed over a bowl. Repeat with the remaining potatoes. Leave the oil in the pan.

2 Add the onion and leek to the frying pan and cook, stirring often, until tender, about 12 minutes. Using the slotted spoon, transfer the onion and leek to the colander with the potatoes.

3 In a large bowl, whisk the eggs until well blended. Add the potatoes, onion, and leek, and stir together gently.

4 Pour all but about 2 tbsp of the oil from the frying pan into a small bowl and set aside. Warm the oil remaining in the pan over medium-low heat. Add the potato-onion mixture and, using a spatula, form the mixture into a thick disk. Cook, shaking the pan back and forth occasionally to keep the tortilla from sticking, until the bottom is golden brown, 8–10 minutes. Invert a large round plate on top of the pan, carefully invert the pan and plate together, then lift off the pan. Add 1–2 tbsp of the reserved olive oil to the pan. Slide the tortilla back into the pan and return it to medium-low heat. Cook until the other side is set, 4–6 minutes.

5 Slide the tortilla onto a plate. Let stand until slightly cooled, at least 10 minutes. Cut into wedges and serve warm or at room temperature.

Known as *caponata* in Sicily, this tangy dish is the perfect snack for a hot summer day. Serve over slices of toasted or grilled bread.

Sweet-and-Sour Eggplant

2 tbsp capers, preferably salt-packed

¼ cup (2 fl oz/60 ml) olive oil

1 yellow onion, chopped

1 eggplant, about 1½ lb (750 g), peeled and cut into cubes

1 clove garlic, minced

1 rib celery, sliced

½ cup (4 fl oz/125 ml) tomato sauce, homemade (page 284) or purchased

6 green olives, pitted and chopped

2 tbsp pine nuts, lightly toasted (page 290), plus extra for garnish

Salt and freshly ground pepper

¼ cup (2 fl oz/60 ml) red wine vinegar

3 tbsp sugar

MAKES 6 SERVINGS

1 Place the capers in a small bowl with cold water to cover and soak for 20 minutes. Drain, rinse well, and drain again. Pat dry on paper towels. Or, if using vinegar-packed capers, rinse under cold running water, drain, and pat dry. Chop the capers and set aside.

2 In a large frying pan over medium-high heat, warm the olive oil. Add the onion and sauté until lightly browned, about 8 minutes. Mix in the eggplant and cook, stirring occasionally, until the eggplant is soft and lightly browned, about 15 minutes. Add the garlic, celery, tomato sauce, and ½ cup (4 fl oz/ 125 ml) water. Cook, stirring occasionally, until the eggplant is very soft, about 5 minutes. Mix in the capers, olives, and pine nuts. Season to taste with salt and pepper. Remove from the heat.

3 In a small saucepan over medium heat, bring the vinegar and sugar almost to a boil. When the sugar dissolves, after about 2 minutes, pour the warm liquid over the eggplant mixture. Return the mixture to medium heat and cook until the liquid is absorbed, 1–2 minutes. Remove from the heat and let stand at room temperature for at least 2 hours or in the refrigerator up to overnight to allow the flavors to blend before serving at room temperature.

This garlicky Spanish appetizer is a snap to make. Serve the shrimp piping hot with plenty of crusty bread to dip into the sauce.

Shrimp with
Garlic & Olive Oil

1 lb (500 g) medium shrimp, peeled and deveined (page 292) with tail segments intact

Salt and freshly ground black pepper

2 tbsp olive oil

4 cloves garlic, minced

1 leek, white part only, finely chopped

¼ tsp red pepper flakes

2 tbsp dry white wine

1 tbsp minced fresh flat-leaf parsley

MAKES 4–6 SERVINGS

1 Season the shrimp with 1 tsp salt. Warm a large, heavy frying pan over medium-high heat until hot. Add the shrimp and cook, turning once, just until they turn pink, about 1 minute on each side.

2 Add the oil, garlic, leek, and red pepper flakes to the pan with the shrimp. Sauté until the shrimp are fully curled, 1–2 minutes longer. Add the wine and cook until it has almost evaporated and the shrimp are opaque throughout, about 1 minute. Transfer the contents of the pan to a serving plate. Taste and adjust the seasoning with salt and black pepper. Garnish with the parsley and serve.

This Lebanese salad features toasted pita, fresh vegetables, and a tart-sweet dressing made from pomegranate juice.

Middle Eastern
Flatbread Salad

1 pita bread, 8 inches (20 cm) in diameter

1 large, ripe tomato, chopped

¾ cup (2 oz/60 g) chopped green onions

½ English cucumber, peeled, quartered lengthwise, seeded, and sliced

½ cup (¾ oz/20 g) coarsely chopped fresh flat-leaf parsley

2 tbsp pomegranate juice

1 tbsp red wine vinegar

2 tbsp olive oil

Salt and freshly ground pepper

MAKES 4 SERVINGS

1 Preheat the oven to 325°F (165°C). Separate the pita bread into 2 rounds. Place both pieces on the oven rack and toast until crisp but not browned, 3–4 minutes. Set aside to cool.

2 In a large serving bowl, combine the tomato, green onions, cucumber, and parsley and toss to mix.

3 To make the dressing, in a small bowl, whisk together the pomegranate juice, vinegar, and olive oil. Season to taste with salt and pepper.

4 Just before serving, break the pita bread into 1-inch (2.5-cm) pieces. Drizzle the dressing over the salad, add the pita pieces, and toss to coat evenly. Serve at once.

Tabbouleh Salad

1 cup (8 fl oz/250 ml) boiling water

½ cup (3 oz/90 g) fine bulgur

1½ cups (2 oz/60 g) minced fresh flat-leaf parsley

⅔ cup (1 oz/30 g) minced fresh mint

½ cup (2½ oz/75 g) finely chopped red onion

2 cups (12 oz/375 g) cherry tomatoes, halved

Juice of 1 large lemon

2 tbsp olive oil

Salt and freshly ground pepper

MAKES 4 SERVINGS

1 In a large bowl, pour the boiling water over the bulgur. Let stand for about 30 minutes, uncovered, until the bulgur has absorbed all of the liquid and has softened. Add the parsley, mint, onion, and cherry tomatoes to the bulgur and mix with a fork to combine.

2 Drizzle the lemon juice and olive oil over the tabbouleh and mix well with the fork. Season to taste with salt and pepper. Cover and refrigerate for at least 2 hours or up to 24 hours before serving.

Bulgur labeled "fine" will marry best with the other ingredients in this iconic Middle Eastern salad.

Greek Salad

1½ lb (750 g) ripe tomatoes, cut into cubes

½ cup (¾ oz/20 g) torn fresh basil leaves

2 tbsp olive oil

½ tsp minced garlic

Salt and freshly ground pepper

6-inch (15-cm) piece English cucumber

½ sweet onion such as Walla Walla, Maui, or Vidalia

½ cup (2½ oz/75 g) crumbled feta or *ricotta salata* cheese

2 tbsp sliced pitted Kalamata olives

1 tsp red wine vinegar

MAKES 4–6 SERVINGS

1 In a large bowl, combine the tomatoes, basil, olive oil, garlic, and ¼ tsp salt and toss gently to mix. Let stand for 5 minutes.

2 Cut the cucumber in half lengthwise, remove and discard the seeds, then cut into ½-inch (12-mm) cubes. Coarsely chop the onion.

3 Add the cucumber, onion, cheese, and olives to the tomato mixture, then sprinkle with the vinegar and toss to mix. Season with pepper and stir to blend. Serve the salad at room temperature.

This crisp salad is delicious even without any lettuce, getting its satisfying crunch from bright green cucumbers instead.

Fruit-and-nut-studded couscous goes well with almost any Middle Eastern tagine or stew as well as grilled or roasted meats.

Couscous with Apricots & Almonds

2 tbsp olive oil

2 cups (12 oz/375 g) couscous

⅓ cup (2 oz/60 g) dried apricot halves, finely slivered

2⅔ cups (21 fl oz/645 ml) chicken stock, homemade (page 283) or purchased

½ tsp ground turmeric

Salt and freshly ground pepper

⅔ cup (3 oz/90 g) slivered almonds, toasted (page 290)

¼ cup (1½ oz/45 g) dried currants

1 tsp finely grated orange zest

2 tbsp fresh lemon juice

½ cup (¾ oz/20 g) minced fresh mint

MAKES 4–6 SERVINGS

1 In a large bowl, drizzle the olive oil over the couscous and toss to coat thoroughly. Scatter the apricots over the couscous.

2 In a small saucepan, bring the stock to a boil over medium-high heat. Stir in the turmeric and ¼ tsp salt, then pour the stock mixture over the couscous. Cover the bowl tightly with aluminum foil and let stand until the couscous has absorbed all the liquid and has softened, about 5 minutes.

3 Remove the foil and fluff the grains with a fork. Stir in the almonds, currants, orange zest, lemon juice, and mint. Season to taste with salt and pepper. Mound the couscous in a serving bowl and serve at once.

Spinach, feta, and filo are all familiar ingredients in Greek cuisine. Here, they combine in a flaky, savory pie.

Greek Spinach & Feta Pie

5 tbsp (3 fl oz/80 ml) olive oil

½ cup (1½ oz/45 g) chopped green onions

2 lb (1 kg) spinach, cooked and finely chopped (page 287)

⅓ cup (2½ oz/75 g) small-curd cottage cheese

½ cup (2½ oz/75 g) crumbled feta cheese

¼ cup (⅓ oz/10 g) *each* minced fresh dill and minced fresh flat-leaf parsley

1 egg, beaten

⅛ tsp freshly grated nutmeg

Salt and freshly ground pepper

16 sheets filo dough, thawed if frozen

MAKES 6 SERVINGS

1 Preheat the oven to 350°F (180°C). Have ready an 8-inch (20-cm) square baking dish, preferably glass.

2 In a frying pan over medium-high heat, warm 1 tbsp of the olive oil. Add the green onions and cook, stirring often, until softened, about 3 minutes. Transfer the contents of the pan to a large bowl and add the spinach, cottage cheese, feta cheese, dill, parsley, egg, and nutmeg. Using a fork, toss to combine well. Season to taste with salt and pepper.

3 To assemble the pie, lay the filo on a dry kitchen towel to one side of your work surface. Cover with a sheet of plastic wrap, then a dampened kitchen towel. Place 1 sheet of the dough in front of you. Brush it lightly with some of the remaining olive oil, working from the edges to the center. Layer 7 more sheets of the dough over the first, lightly oiling each one. Using a sharp knife, trim the stacked sheets of dough into an 8½-inch (21.5-cm) square. Fit the dough stack to cover the bottom and slightly up the sides of the baking dish.

4 Spoon the filling into the pan to cover the filo. Using the remaining filo, make another stack of 8 sheets on your work surface in the same way and trim it into an 8-inch (20-cm) square. Place the second stack to cover the spinach filling. Using the sharp knife, cut through the pie, dividing it in half. Turn the pan 90 degrees and cut the pie into thirds to make 6 pieces.

5 Bake until the filo is crisp and golden, about 45 minutes. Transfer to a wire rack and let cool for about 20 minutes. Serve warm, cut into rectangles.

Pistachio Baklava

1½ cups (6 oz/185 g) shelled raw pistachios

1 cup (4 oz/125 g) walnuts

¾ cup (6 oz/185 g) plus 3 tbsp sugar

1 tsp ground cinnamon

¼ tsp ground cloves

Salt

1 lb (500 g) filo dough, thawed if frozen and cut in half lengthwise

½ cup (4 oz/125 g) unsalted butter, melted

1 cup (12 oz/375 g) honey

MAKES 24 PIECES

1 In a food processor, combine the pistachios, walnuts, 3 tbsp sugar, cinnamon, cloves, and ¼ tsp salt. Pulse until finely ground. Transfer the mixture to a bowl and set aside.

2 Pile the filo dough sheets in a single stack on a dry kitchen towel. Cover with a sheet of plastic wrap, then a dampened kitchen towel. Brush a 9-by-13-inch (23-by-33-cm) baking dish lightly with some of the melted butter. Place 1 sheet of filo in the dish and brush it lightly with some of the melted butter, working from the edges to the center. Repeat to make 12 layers. Sprinkle about one-fourth of the nut mixture evenly over the top sheet, then top with 2 more buttered filo sheets. Repeat twice more, then finish with the remaining one-fourth of the nut mixture and all of the remaining filo (about 12 sheets), again brushing each with butter. Brush the top sheet generously with the remaining butter and refrigerate the dish for 15 minutes.

3 Preheat the oven to 350°F (180°C). Using a thin, serrated knife, cut the baklava into approximately 24 squares. Bake until golden brown, about 50 minutes. Transfer to a wire rack and let cool slightly.

4 In a saucepan over medium heat, combine the ¾ cup sugar with ½ cup (4 fl oz/125 ml) water and bring to a boil, stirring to dissolve the sugar. Boil, without stirring, until the mixture registers 220°F (105°C) on a candy thermometer, 4–5 minutes. Remove from the heat and stir in the honey.

5 Pour the honey syrup evenly over the warm baklava. Cover loosely with waxed paper and let stand at room temperature for at least 8 hours or up to overnight, then serve.

Almond Torte

Butter for greasing

1½ cups (7½ oz/235 g) flour, plus extra for dusting

2 tsp baking powder

Salt

½ cup (2½ oz/75 g) coarsely chopped blanched almonds

1 cup (8 oz/250 g) sugar

3 eggs

⅓ cup (3 fl oz/80 ml) olive oil

Finely grated zest of 1 orange

2 tsp pure vanilla extract

Orange segments (page 290), pomegranate seeds, and honey for garnish (optional)

MAKES 8 SERVINGS

1 Preheat the oven to 350°F (180°C). Butter a 9-inch (23-cm) springform pan. Dust with flour and shake out the excess.

2 In a bowl, stir together the flour, baking powder, and ½ tsp salt. In a food processor, process the almonds and ¼ cup (2 oz/60 g) of the sugar until the almonds are finely ground.

3 In a large bowl, using an electric mixer set on medium-high speed, beat the eggs until frothy. Add the remaining ¾ cup (6 oz/190 g) sugar and beat at high speed until the mixture is thick and pale yellow, 6–8 minutes. On low speed, beat in the olive oil, orange zest, and vanilla. Using a rubber spatula, gently fold the flour and almond mixtures into the egg mixture until well blended. Scrape the batter into the prepared pan.

4 Bake the torte until the top is golden brown and a toothpick inserted into the center comes out clean, about 30 minutes. Let cool in the pan on a wire rack for 10 minutes. Run a thin-bladed knife around the edge of the pan to loosen the torte sides and remove the pan sides. Let cool completely.

5 Serve slices on individual plates garnished with orange segments and pomegranate seeds and drizzled with honey, if desired.

Mexican

The addition of bright, tart fruit such as fresh mango and pomegranate seeds brings a fresh twist to this always-popular dip.

Guacamole with Mango & Pomegranate

3 ripe avocados

2 tsp fresh lime juice

Salt

¼ small white onion, finely chopped

1 small serrano chile, seeded and minced

3 sprigs fresh cilantro, stemmed and finely chopped

2 tbsp chopped mango (page 212)

2 tbsp pomegranate seeds

½ small plum tomato, cored, seeded (page 290), and finely chopped

Tortilla chips for serving

MAKES 4 SERVINGS

1 Cut the avocados in half and remove the pits. Scoop the flesh into a bowl. Using a fork or a potato masher, mash the avocados with the lime juice and ½ tsp salt until the guacamole is smooth but still has a little texture. Stir in the onion, chile, and cilantro. Taste and adjust the seasoning.

2 Spoon the guacamole into a serving bowl. Scatter the mango, pomegranate seeds, and tomato on top. Serve with the tortilla chips.

NOTE For a classic version of guacamole, omit the pomegranate and mango, and garnish with 1 tbsp chopped fresh cilantro leaves, crumbled *cotija* or feta cheese, or toasted pumpkin seeds.

These Mexican grilled cheese "sandwiches" are always a crowd-pleaser. Try using other fillings such as sautéed chicken or mushrooms.

Chile-Cheese Quesadillas

3 tbsp canola oil, or as needed

1 white onion, thinly sliced

2 cloves garlic, minced

½ tsp dried oregano

2 poblano chiles, roasted (page 291) and seeded, then cut lengthwise into 12 strips

Salt

8 corn tortillas

½ lb (250 g) Monterey jack or Muenster cheese, shredded

2 tbsp minced fresh cilantro

Guacamole, homemade (page 138) or purchased, for serving

Salsa Fresca (page 284), Tomatillo-Avocado Salsa, (page 285), or purchased salsa for serving

MAKES 4 SERVINGS

1 In a large frying pan over medium heat, warm 1 tbsp of the oil. Add the onion and sauté until golden, about 5 minutes. Stir in the garlic and oregano and continue cooking for 1 minute. Add the chiles and ½ tsp salt and stir until heated through, about 1 minute longer. Transfer to a bowl and set aside.

2 Spread the tortillas on a work surface. For each tortilla, sprinkle a generous tablespoonful of the shredded cheese on half of the tortilla, keeping the edges free. Top with a sprinkle of cilantro and a spoonful of the chile-onion mixture. Fold the uncovered side of the tortilla over the filling.

3 Preheat the oven to 200°F (95°C). Line a heatproof serving platter with paper towels and place in the oven. In the large frying pan over medium heat, warm 1 tbsp of the oil. Working in batches, fry the quesadillas, turning once, until golden on both sides, about 3 minutes. Using a spatula, transfer each quesadilla to the serving platter in the oven. Repeat with the remaining quesadillas, adding more oil to the pan as needed. Serve at once with the guacamole and salsa on the side.

Here, acidic lime juice "cooks" the raw fish.
Olives add brininess and avocados a cool
and creamy contrast to the overall flavor.

Halibut, Lime
& Avocado Ceviche

1¼ lb (625 g) halibut
or other white fish fillets

½ cup (4 fl oz/125 ml)
fresh lime juice

2 firm but ripe tomatoes, peeled,
seeded (page 290), and diced

2 serrano chiles, seeded
and minced

⅓ cup (½ oz/15 g) minced
fresh cilantro

Salt and freshly ground pepper

1 avocado

10 green olives such as
Manzanilla, pitted and
coarsely chopped

1 tsp dried oregano

2 tbsp olive oil

Tortilla chips for serving
(optional)

MAKES 6 SERVINGS

1 Cut the fish fillets into small cubes and put them in a large nonreactive
bowl. Pour the lime juice over the fish, making sure all the pieces are evenly
covered. Cover with plastic wrap, place in the refrigerator, and let the fish
marinate for 3–4 hours.

2 Drain the fish, discarding the lime juice, and pat dry with paper towels.
Put the fish back into the bowl and add the tomatoes, chiles, cilantro, and
salt and pepper to taste. Stir gently to blend and refrigerate for at least
2 hours or up to 12 hours.

3 When ready to serve, halve, pit, and dice the avocado (page 290) and
stir it into the fish mixture along with the olives and oregano. Drizzle the
ceviche with the olive oil and spoon into 6 individual glasses. Serve at
once with tortilla chips, if desired.

Shrimp-Stuffed Avocados

¼ cup (2 oz/185 g) ketchup

2 tbsp finely chopped
white onion

1 tbsp minced fresh cilantro

1 tbsp olive oil

1 tbsp fresh lime juice

2 tsp Worcestershire sauce

¼ tsp seeded and minced
habanero chile (optional)

⅓ lb (155 g) cooked bay shrimp
(about 1 cup)

2 ripe but firm avocados

MAKES 4 SERVINGS

1 In a nonreactive bowl, combine the ketchup, onion, cilantro, olive oil, lime juice, Worcestershire sauce, and habanero, if using, and stir with a fork to mix well. Add the shrimp and stir to coat thoroughly with the sauce. Cover and refrigerate until well chilled.

2 Using a large, sharp knife, cut each avocado in half lengthwise, cutting down and around the pit. Hold the avocado so that one of the halves rests in each hand. Gently rotate in opposite directions to separate the halves. Holding the avocado half with the pit in one hand, strike the pit with the heel of the knife blade, lodging it into the pit. Twist the knife carefully to lift out the pit.

3 Spoon the shrimp into the hollow of each avocado half and serve at once.

Tiny bay shrimp are brightened
with lime juice and cilantro in this
refreshing and eye-catching salad.

Stuffed Poblano Chiles

¼ cup (2 fl oz/60 ml) olive oil

⅓ cup (2 oz/60 g) raisins

⅓ cup (2 oz/60 g) pine nuts, lightly toasted (page 290)

2½ lb (1.25 kg) spinach, cooked and chopped (page 287)

6 whole poblano chiles, roasted and peeled (page 291)

6 oz (185 g) Monterey jack cheese, thinly sliced

Roasted Tomato Sauce (page 284)

½ cup (4 oz/125 g) *crema* or sour cream thinned with 2 tbsp water (optional)

MAKES 6 SERVINGS

1 Preheat the oven to 350°F (180°C). In a large frying pan over medium-high heat, warm the oil. Add the raisins, pine nuts, and spinach and cook, stirring constantly, until the spinach is wilted and the mixture is dry, about 3 minutes. Pour in ½ cup (4 fl oz/125 ml) water and continue to stir until evaporated, about 5 minutes. Remove from the heat; let cool.

2 Leaving the stem end intact, make a lengthwise slit in each chile and remove the seeds and veins. Divide the spinach mixture and cheese slices among the chiles, stuffing them carefully so as not to tear them and allowing them to close completely with overlapping edges. Place the stuffed chiles in a shallow baking dish and cover with aluminum foil. Bake until heated through and the cheese is softened, 20–30 minutes.

3 Meanwhile, warm the tomato sauce in a saucepan over medium-low heat. Spread the warm sauce evenly onto the bottom of a serving platter. Remove the chiles from the oven and arrange them on the platter. Drizzle with the *crema*, if using, and serve at once.

Mild, meaty poblano chiles are filled with a savory combination of cheese and spinach for a hearty starter.

The zesty tomatillo salsa helps balance the richness of this hearty dish. Serve with black beans for a Mexican-inspired brunch.

Chilaquiles with Poached Eggs

2 cups (16 fl oz/500 ml) canola oil

12 corn tortillas, torn into strips

½ small yellow onion, chopped

1 cup (8 fl oz/250 ml) Tomatillo-Avocado Salsa (page 285) made without avocados, or purchased tomatillo salsa

1 cup (4 oz/125 g) shredded Monterey jack cheese

1 tbsp minced fresh oregano

1 tsp fresh lemon juice

4–6 eggs

Salt and freshly ground pepper

1 cup (5 oz/155 g) crumbled *queso fresco* or feta cheese

MAKES 4–6 SERVINGS

1 In a heavy frying pan over medium-high heat, warm the oil. Working in batches, add the tortilla strips and fry until golden on one side, about 30 seconds. Turn and fry until golden on the other side, 15–20 seconds. Transfer the strips to paper towels to drain.

2 Pour off all but 1–2 tbsp of the oil from the pan and place over medium heat. Add the onion and cook, stirring, until translucent, about 1 minute. Add the tortilla strips and tomatillo salsa and cook, stirring gently, until the tortillas are softened, 3–4 minutes. Stir in the jack cheese and the oregano. Continue to cook until the cheese has melted, 4–5 minutes longer.

3 To poach the eggs, pour water to a depth of 2 inches (5 cm) into a large saucepan and add the lemon juice. Place over medium heat and bring to a gentle simmer. Break an egg into a small bowl and gently slide the egg into the simmering water. Repeat with the remaining eggs, spacing them apart. Cook until the whites are set, about 5 minutes.

4 Just before the eggs are done, divide the warm chilaquiles among warmed individual plates. Using a slotted spoon, lift each egg from the simmering water, letting the excess water drain into the saucepan. Top each serving with a poached egg. Season to taste with salt and pepper. Sprinkle with *queso fresco* and serve at once.

Translated as "ranch eggs," this popular dish was traditionally served as a mid-morning meal to hungry farmhands.

Huevos Rancheros

1 cup (6 oz/185 g) canned diced tomatoes, drained

2 serrano chiles, seeded and minced

½ small white onion, chopped

1 clove garlic

¼ cup (2 fl oz/60 ml) plus 1 tbsp canola oil

Salt and freshly ground pepper

4 large, thick corn tortillas, preferably stale

4 eggs

1 cup (8 oz/250 g) refried beans, homemade (page 170) or purchased, warmed

⅔ cup (5 oz/155 g) sour cream

½ cup (2½ oz/75 g) crumbled *queso fresco* or feta cheese

1 tbsp chopped fresh cilantro

1 small avocado, halved, pitted, and diced (page 290)

MAKES 4 SERVINGS

1 In a food processor, process the tomatoes, chiles, onion, and garlic until blended but still chunky. In a large frying pan over medium-high heat, warm the 1 tbsp oil. Add the tomato mixture and cook, stirring constantly, until thickened, about 5 minutes. Stir in ½ tsp salt and pepper to taste. Remove from the heat and cover to keep warm.

2 Preheat the oven to 200°F (95°C). Have ready a paper towel–lined baking sheet. In a large frying pan over medium-high heat, warm the remaining ¼ cup (2 fl oz/60 ml) oil. One at a time, fry the tortillas, turning once, until softened, about 5 seconds on each side. Using tongs, transfer to the baking sheet to drain. Place in the oven to keep warm.

3 Reduce the heat to medium-low and wait a few minutes for the frying pan to cool down. Break the eggs into the pan, spacing them evenly, and fry until the whites are set, about 5 minutes. Season to taste with salt and pepper.

4 Remove the tortillas from the oven. Using tongs, dip each tortilla quickly in the warm tomato salsa and place on warmed individual plates. Spread the warm refried beans on each tortilla, dividing evenly, and top each with a fried egg. Spoon more of the tomato salsa generously over each serving. Drizzle with sour cream, then sprinkle with the cheese, cilantro, and diced avocado. Serve at once.

Earthy tomato-chile broth thickened with a corn tortilla makes a satisfying base for toppings like cheese, avocado, and chile.

Tortilla Soup

6 corn tortillas

2 ancho chiles, seeded and deveined (page 291)

7 tbsp (3½ fl oz/105 ml) canola oil

½ white onion, chopped

2 cloves garlic

1 large ripe tomato, coarsely chopped, or 1 can (8 oz/250 g) chopped tomatoes, drained

6 cups (48 fl oz/1.5 l) chicken stock, homemade (page 283) or purchased

¼ tsp dried oregano

1 tbsp chopped fresh cilantro

Salt

¼ lb (125 g) *queso fresco* cheese, crumbled, or Monterey jack cheese, shredded

1 avocado, halved, pitted, and diced (page 290)

MAKES 6 SERVINGS

1 Set 1 tortilla aside. Cut the other tortillas in half and then cut crosswise into strips ½ inch (12 mm) wide. Let them dry for 5–10 minutes. In a bowl, soak 1 of the chiles in hot water for 10–15 minutes. Cut the other chile lengthwise into thin strips about 1 inch (2.5 cm) long.

2 Have ready a paper towel–lined baking sheet. In a frying pan over medium-high heat, warm 6 tbsp (3 fl oz/90 ml) of the oil. When it is hot, add the tortilla strips and fry, tossing, until crisp and golden on both sides, about 5 seconds. Using a slotted spoon, transfer to the lined baking sheet. Fry the chile strips very quickly in the same oil, again for about 5 seconds, then transfer to the baking sheet.

3 Pour off all but 1 tbsp of the oil from the pan and place over medium-low heat. Add the onion and garlic and sauté until golden brown, 10–12 minutes. Transfer to a blender or food processor. Drain the soaked chile, discarding the soaking liquid. Tear the chile and remaining tortilla into pieces and add to the blender or food processor along with the tomato. Purée until smooth, adding up to ¼ cup (2 fl oz/60 ml) water if needed.

4 In a Dutch oven or large, heavy pot over medium-high heat, warm the remaining 1 tbsp oil. Add the chile-tomato purée and cook, stirring often, until it deepens in color, 5–6 minutes. Stir in the stock, oregano, and cilantro and simmer to blend the flavors, about 15 minutes. Season to taste with salt.

5 Divide half of the tortilla strips among warmed individual bowls, then ladle the hot soup into the bowls. Top with the remaining tortilla strips and the cheese, chile strips, and diced avocado. Serve at once.

Pork & Hominy Soup

3 lb (1.5 kg) boneless pork shoulder, trimmed of excess fat and cut into chunks

4 cans (15½ oz/485 g each) white hominy, drained, rinsed, and drained again

3 yellow onions, finely chopped

6 cloves garlic, minced

4 cups (32 fl oz/1 l) chicken stock, homemade (page 283) or purchased

4 tbsp chile powder

1 tbsp dried oregano

1½ tsp ground cumin

Salt and freshly ground pepper

½ small head green cabbage

1 small bunch red radishes

2 ripe avocados

3 limes, cut into wedges

MAKES 8–10 SERVINGS

1 Place the pork, hominy, two-thirds of the onions, the garlic, stock, chile powder, oregano, cumin, 1½ tsp salt, and ½ tsp pepper in a Dutch oven or slow cooker. Stir to combine. If using a Dutch oven, bring to a boil over medium-high heat, reduce the heat to very low, partially cover, and cook until the pork is very tender, about 3 hours. If using a slow cooker, cover and cook for 4 hours on the high-heat setting or 8 hours on the low-heat setting.

2 While the soup is cooking, halve, core, and finely shred the cabbage. Thinly slice the radishes and cut into matchsticks. Halve, pit, and dice the avocados (page 290). Arrange the cabbage, radishes, avocado, lime wedges, and remaining onions in small bowls.

3 Season the soup to taste with salt and pepper. Ladle into warmed bowls and serve at once. Pass the accompaniments at the table.

Posole, a slowly simmered, hearty soup, is favored in kitchens in both Mexico and the U.S. Southwest.

Corn & Chile Chowder

8 cups (64 fl oz/2 l) whole milk

1–2 dried chipotle chiles, seeded and chopped

2 bay leaves

2 tbsp unsalted butter

2 tbsp olive oil

2 large yellow onions, chopped

Salt

4–6 cloves garlic, minced

1 tbsp ground cumin

Kernels from 8 ears of corn (about 8 cups/4 lb/2kg) (page 292)

6 large poblano chiles, roasted, peeled, and seeded (page 291), then chopped

6 green onions, finely chopped

MAKES 6 SERVINGS

1 In a heavy saucepan over medium-low heat, warm the milk, chipotle chiles, and bay leaves. Bring to a gentle simmer; do not allow to boil. Remove from the heat and let stand, covered, for about 20 minutes.

2 Meanwhile, melt the butter with the olive oil in a stockpot over medium heat. Add the onions and 2 tsp salt and sauté, stirring, until the onions are soft and golden brown, 15–20 minutes. Reduce the heat to medium-low, add the garlic and cumin, and sauté, stirring constantly, until aromatic, about 5 minutes. Stir in the corn and poblano chiles and continue to cook until the corn is lightly browned, about 5 minutes.

3 Using a fine-mesh sieve, strain the warm milk into the corn mixture and simmer until the flavors have blended, about 15 minutes. Remove from the heat and let cool for about 5 minutes.

4 Transfer about one-third of the soup to a food processor or blender and purée until smooth. Return the purée to the pot, stirring well. If necessary, reheat the soup over low heat. Taste and adjust the seasonings. Ladle the soup into warmed bowls, garnish with the green onions, and serve at once.

Juicy jicama and tangy grapefruit refresh, while avocado adds satisfying creaminess to this light warm-weather salad.

Jicama, Grapefruit & Avocado Salad

2 small jicama (about 1 lb/ 500 g total weight)

1 ruby red grapefruit

1 large avocado, halved, pitted, and diced (page 290)

2 tbsp fresh lime juice

1 tbsp fresh orange juice

2 tsp honey

Pinch of cayenne pepper

Salt

¼ cup (⅓ oz/10 g) fresh cilantro leaves

MAKES 4–6 SERVINGS

1 Cut each jicama in half and, using a peeler or a sharp knife, remove the peel. Place the jicama halves cut side down on a cutting board and cut lengthwise into ¼-inch (6-mm) slices. Stack the slices in piles of 3 or 4 and cut each stack in half crosswise at ¼-inch (6-mm) intervals to create matchsticks. If some of the matchsticks seem too long, cut them in half. Place the jicama in a serving bowl.

2 Working over another bowl, segment the grapefruit (page 290), letting the juice drop into the bowl. Reserve 2 tbsp of the juice for the dressing. Add the grapefruit and the diced avocado to the bowl with the jicama.

3 To make the dressing, in a small bowl, stir together the reserved grapefruit juice, the lime juice, orange juice, honey, cayenne, and salt to taste. Mix well to dissolve the honey completely. Pour about half of the dressing over the salad and toss gently. Taste, then add more dressing and salt as necessary. Garnish the salad with the cilantro leaves, and serve at once.

In the Gulf of Mexico, anglers regularly reel in red snapper, a fish with firm flesh and a mild, sweet flavor—perfect for tacos.

Fish Tacos with Tomatillo Salsa

½ lb (250 g) tomatillos, husks removed, rinsed, and finely chopped

1 jalapeño chile, seeded and minced

¾ cup (1 oz/30 g) minced fresh cilantro

2 tbsp fresh lime juice

1 tsp sugar

2 tbsp olive oil, plus extra for brushing

Salt

½ small head green cabbage, core intact, cut into slices ½ inch (12 mm) thick

1½ lb (750 g) red snapper fillets

12 corn tortillas

1 large avocado, halved, pitted, and sliced (page 290) and sprinkled with lemon juice

8 radishes, grated

MAKES 6 SERVINGS

1 About 2 hours before grilling, make the salsa. In a bowl, stir together the tomatillos, jalapeño, cilantro, lime juice, sugar, and 2 tbsp oil until the sugar is dissolved and the ingredients are well mixed. Season to taste with salt. Cover and refrigerate until ready to serve.

2 Prepare a gas or charcoal grill for direct grilling over medium-high heat (page 293). Oil the grill rack. Brush the cabbage and fish on both sides with oil. Divide the tortillas into two stacks and wrap each stack in aluminum foil.

3 Place the cabbage slices and fish fillets directly over the heat elements or over the hottest part of the fire. Cover the grill and cook, turning both the fish and the cabbage once. The fish is ready when it is opaque throughout and flakes when prodded with a fork, 6–8 minutes, and the cabbage is ready when it is fork-tender, 10–12 minutes. About 3 minutes before the fish and cabbage are done, place the packets of tortillas on a lower-heat area of the grill to warm, turning once.

4 Working quickly, remove the fish, cabbage, and tortillas from the grill. Chop the cabbage and cut the fish into smaller pieces, then fill each tortilla with equal amounts of the chopped cabbage and fish, avocado, radishes, and tomatillo salsa. Put the extra chopped cabbage and any remaining salsa in separate dishes and pass at the table. Serve at once.

Fish Baked with
Garlic & Tomatoes

12 cloves garlic

2 tsp fresh lime juice

Salt and freshly ground pepper

6 skinless red snapper fillets,
about 6 oz (185 g) each

¼ cup (2 fl oz/60 ml) olive oil

1 large white onion, thinly sliced

3 lb (1.5 kg) ripe tomatoes,
roasted, peeled (page 290),
and finely chopped

3 pickled jalapeño chiles,
with 1 tbsp pickling liquid

½ cup (3 oz/90 g) small
green pimiento-stuffed
olives, chopped

½ cup (¾ oz/20 g) chopped
fresh flat-leaf parsley leaves

3 bay leaves

1 tbsp capers

½ tsp *each* dried oregano,
marjoram, and thyme

MAKES 4–6 SERVINGS

1 Using a mortar and pestle, mash 8 cloves of garlic to a paste, or squeeze the cloves through a garlic press. Transfer to a small bowl. Add the lime juice and ½ tsp salt and mix well. Lightly oil a large glass or ceramic baking dish and place the fish fillets in the dish. Rub the garlic mixture over both sides of each fillet. Cover with plastic wrap and let marinate in the refrigerator, turning occasionally, for at least 30 minutes or up to 2 hours.

2 Preheat the oven to 350°F (180°C). Mince the remaining 4 garlic cloves. In a large, heavy frying pan over medium heat, warm the olive oil. Add the onion and sauté until soft, about 4 minutes. Add the minced garlic and continue cooking until golden, 1–2 minutes. Raise the heat to medium-high, add the tomatoes, and continue cooking, stirring frequently, until the sauce thickens, 5–7 minutes. Cut the jalapeños lengthwise into strips. Reduce the heat to low and stir in the jalapeños and pickling liquid, olives, parsley, bay leaves, and capers. Add the oregano, marjoram, and thyme and season to taste with salt and pepper. Simmer, stirring occasionally, until the flavors are well blended, 8–10 minutes.

3 Unwrap the fish and spoon the sauce evenly over the top, discarding the bay leaves. Bake, basting occasionally with the sauce, just until the flesh is opaque throughout, 8–10 minutes. Serve at once directly from the baking dish or, using 2 spatulas, carefully transfer to a warmed platter.

Chicken with Pumpkin Seed Mole

¼ cup (2 fl oz/60 ml) olive oil

1 white onion, chopped

2 cloves garlic, chopped

2 jalapeño chiles, seeded and coarsely chopped

1½ cups (6 oz/185 g) pumpkin seeds

1½ cups (12 fl oz/375 ml) chicken stock, homemade (page 283) or purchased

¾ lb (375 g) tomatillos, husks removed, rinsed, and chopped

¾ cup (¾ oz/20 g) loosely packed fresh cilantro leaves, plus extra for garnish

1 tsp dried oregano

Salt

3 lb (1.5 kg) skinless, boneless chicken thighs

Steamed Rice (page 288) for serving

¼ cup (2 oz/60 g) sour cream

MAKES 6–8 SERVINGS

1 In a Dutch oven or large, heavy pot over medium-high heat, warm the oil. Add the onion and sauté until it starts to turn tender, about 3 minutes. Stir in the garlic and jalapeños and sauté for about 30 seconds. Add the pumpkin seeds and cook, stirring, until they darken in color, about 5 minutes. Stir in the stock, tomatillos, cilantro, oregano, and 1 tsp salt. Bring the mixture to a boil, then remove from the heat.

2 Ladle about half of the pumpkin-seed mixture into a blender or food processor and pulse a few times. Add the remaining mixture and process until it forms a uniformly coarse purée.

3 Return the purée to the pot and add the chicken thighs, spooning some of the puree over the top. Partially cover the pot and cook over low heat until the chicken is opaque throughout and tender, about 1 hour.

4 Divide the steamed rice between warmed individual plates or shallow bowls and top with the chicken and pumpkin seed mole. Garnish with cilantro and sour cream and serve at once.

In these spicy tacos topped with smoky salsa and creamy avocado, you can swap the steak for chicken, if you prefer.

Grilled Steak Tacos with Avocado

½ cup (4 fl oz/125 ml) canola oil

1 yellow onion, thinly sliced

2 cloves garlic, minced

1 jalapeño chile, seeded and minced

1 tbsp minced fresh oregano

1 tsp ground cumin

1 tbsp chili powder

2 tbsp minced fresh cilantro

1 tbsp tequila

Salt

2½–3 lb (1.25–1.5 kg) skirt steak or flank steak, trimmed of fat and silver skin

12 corn tortillas

Chipotle Chile Salsa (page 285) or purchased salsa

2 avocados, halved, pitted, and sliced (page 290)

MAKES 4–6 SERVINGS

1 In a small bowl, mix together the oil, onion, garlic, jalapeño, oregano, cumin, chili powder, cilantro, tequila, and 1½ tsp salt. Put the marinade in a zippered plastic bag. Score the steak a few times across the grain. (If using skirt steak, cut it into 2–4 pieces for easy grilling.) Add the steak to the marinade, seal the bag, and massage to coat the steak with the mixture. Let stand in the refrigerator for at least 6 hours or up to overnight. Remove from the refrigerator about 30 minutes before grilling.

2 Prepare a gas or charcoal grill for direct grilling over high heat (page 293). Oil the grill rack. Remove the steak from the marinade, pat dry, and discard the marinade. Place the steak directly over the heat elements or over the hottest part of the fire. Grill, turning once, until well browned, 7–8 minutes for skirt steak or 9–10 for flank steak. (Move the steak to a cooler part of the grill if flare-ups occur.) The steak is best if not cooked past medium-rare, as these cuts toughen when cooked longer. Transfer the meat to a platter, cover loosely with aluminum foil, and let rest for about 15 minutes.

3 While the steak is resting, divide the tortillas in half and wrap each stack in aluminum foil. Place the packets of tortillas on a lower-heat area of the grill to warm, turning once.

4 Remove the tortillas from the grill. Slice the steak thinly against the grain. To assemble the tacos, place the meat on one side of a tortilla, spoon a little salsa and avocado on top, and fold. Serve at once.

These hearty cheese and chicken enchiladas feature a traditional red sauce, but you can also use purchased green tomatillo sauce.

Chicken Enchiladas

4 tbsp (2 fl oz/60 ml) canola oil

2 cups (16 fl oz/500 ml) Red Chile Sauce (page 284)

1 cup (8 fl oz/250 ml) chicken stock, homemade (page 283) or purchased

Salt

12 corn tortillas, preferably stale

2 cups (12 oz/375 g) Shredded Cooked Chicken (page 288)

2 cups (8 oz/250 g) shredded Monterey jack cheese

½ cup (4 oz/125 g) sour cream

1 small white onion, thinly sliced and separated into rings

6 radishes, trimmed and thinly sliced

MAKES 4–6 SERVINGS

1 Preheat the oven to 325°F (165°C). In a frying pan over medium heat, warm 1 tbsp of the oil. Pour in the chile sauce and cook, stirring, until thickened, about 2 minutes. Add the chicken stock and cook, stirring frequently, until thick, about 5 minutes. Taste and adjust the seasoning with salt. Remove from the heat. Spoon a thin layer of the chile sauce on the bottom of a 9-by-13-inch (23-by-33-cm) baking dish. Set aside.

2 In another frying pan over medium heat, warm the remaining 3 tbsp oil until hot. Using tongs, quickly drag the tortillas one at a time through the oil to soften them on both sides. Drain on a paper towel–lined plate. Pat the tortillas dry with paper towels.

3 In a bowl, mix together the shredded chicken and cheese. Working with one tortilla at a time, spread a spoonful of the chicken-cheese mixture near the edge of the tortilla, roll it up, and place it seam side down in the prepared baking dish. Repeat with the remaining tortillas and chicken-cheese mixture, arranging the rolled tortillas side by side in the dish. Spoon the remaining sauce over the tortillas. Bake the enchiladas until they are heated through and the cheese is melted, about 15 minutes.

4 To serve, top the enchiladas in the pan with the sour cream, onion slices, and radish slices. Serve at once.

Mexican Meatball Soup

¼ cup (1½ oz/45 g) *masa harina*, or ¼ cup (1 oz/30 g) dried bread crumbs

6¼ cups (50 fl oz/1.5 l) chicken stock, homemade (page 283) or purchased

1 lb (500 g) lean ground pork

1 egg

1 yellow onion, finely chopped

4 cloves garlic, minced

1 tbsp chopped fresh oregano

2 tsp ancho chile powder

1½ tsp ground cumin

Salt and freshly ground pepper

2 tbsp canola oil

1½ tsp minced chipotle chiles in adobo sauce

1 can (14½ oz/455 g) diced tomatoes

1 tbsp fresh lime juice

3 tbsp minced fresh cilantro

MAKES 4–6 SERVINGS

1 To make the meatballs, stir together the *masa harina* and ¼ cup (2 fl oz/60 ml) of the chicken stock in a bowl until it forms a paste. Add the pork, egg, half of the onion, half of the garlic, the oregano, chile powder, ½ tsp of the cumin, 1 tsp salt, and ½ tsp pepper. Using your hands, gently but thoroughly blend the ingredients. Form the mixture into small meatballs about 1 inch (2.5 cm) in diameter. Set aside.

2 In a large saucepan over medium heat, warm the oil. Add the remaining onion and sauté until softened and tinged with gold, about 5 minutes. Add the remaining garlic and sauté for 30 seconds. Stir in the remaining 1 tsp cumin and the minced chipotles. Cook, stirring frequently, for 30 seconds, then stir in the remaining 6 cups (48 fl oz/1.5 l) stock and the tomatoes and bring to a simmer.

3 Add the meatballs to the stock mixture and return to a simmer. Cover, reduce the heat to medium-low, and cook, without stirring, until the meatballs are firm, 15–20 minutes.

4 Stir in the lime juice and cilantro. Season to taste with salt and pepper. Ladle into warmed shallow bowls and serve at once.

Chile Verde

4 lb (2 kg) boneless pork shoulder, trimmed of excess fat and cut into cubes

Salt and freshly ground pepper

2 cans (12 oz/375 g each) whole tomatillos, drained

4 cans (7 oz/220 g each) diced, roasted mild green chiles

1 large yellow onion, minced

4 cloves garlic, minced

1 large jalapeño chile, seeded and minced

2 cups (16 fl oz/500 ml) chicken stock, homemade (page 283) or purchased

¾ lb (375 g) firm, ripe tomatoes, finely chopped

1 tbsp dried oregano

2 tsp ground cumin

Toasted corn tortillas, torn into bite-sized pieces, for serving

Sour cream for serving

Minced fresh cilantro for serving

MAKES 8–10 SERVINGS

1 Place the pork in a Dutch oven or slow cooker. Sprinkle with 2 tsp salt and 1 tsp pepper and toss to coat well. Break up the tomatillos with your hands and add to the pork. Add the green chiles, onion, garlic, jalapeño, stock, tomatoes, oregano, and cumin and stir briefly to combine. If using a Dutch oven, bring to a boil over high heat, reduce the heat to very low, partially cover, and cook until the pork is very tender and a thick sauce has formed, 2–3 hours. If using a slow cooker, cover and cook for 4 hours on the high-heat setting or 8 hours on the low-heat setting.

2 Ladle the *chile verde* into warmed bowls and serve at once. Pass the tortillas, sour cream, and cilantro at the table.

This traditional "green chili" stew from Mexico combines lean pork stew meat with mild green chiles and tangy tomatillos.

Here, flavorful pork shoulder is bathed in citrus juice and cooked very slowly until fork tender, making a scrumptious taco or burrito filling.

Carnitas Tacos

Salt and freshly ground pepper

3–4 lb (1.5–2 kg) boneless pork shoulder

¼ cup (2 fl oz/60 ml) olive oil

1 white onion, finely chopped, plus thinly sliced onion for serving

2 cloves garlic, minced

1½ cups (12 fl oz/375 ml) Mexican lager-style beer

Grated zest and juice of 1 large orange

Grated zest and juice of 1 lime, plus 2 limes, cut into wedges, for serving

1 tbsp dried oregano

Salsa Fresca (page 284) or purchased salsa, for serving

2 avocados, halved, pitted, and sliced (page 290)

Warm corn tortillas for serving

MAKES 6–8 SERVINGS

1 Preheat the oven to 350°F (180°C). In a small bowl, combine 2 tsp salt and 1 tsp pepper. Season the pork shoulder with the mixture. Set aside.

2 In a Dutch oven or large, heavy pot over medium-high heat, warm the oil. Add the pork and cook, turning frequently, until browned on all sides, about 10 minutes. Transfer to a large plate and set aside.

3 Pour off all but a thin layer of fat in the pot. Add the chopped onion and garlic and sauté until they begin to soften and become fragrant, 1–2 minutes. Add the beer and deglaze the pot, scraping the bottom with a wooden spoon to dislodge any browned bits.

4 Add the pork to the beer mixture. Add the orange and lime zests and juices and the oregano. Cover, place in the oven, and cook until the pork is very tender, about 2½ hours.

5 Using a slotted spoon, transfer the pork to a cutting board and cover loosely with aluminum foil to keep warm. Using a large spoon, skim as much fat as possible from the surface of the braising liquid. Using a large, sharp knife and a fork, coarsely cut and shred the pork into bite-sized pieces. Arrange the meat on a warmed platter and moisten it with the braising liquid.

6 To serve, put the sliced onion, salsa, avocado slices, and lime wedges in separate bowls. Serve alongside the platter of pork and the warm tortillas, letting diners assemble their own tacos.

In Mexico, smoky grilled corn is often served sprinkled with ground chiles, lime juice, and lashings of cream.

Chile-Lime Corn

6 ears corn, unshucked

2 limes, quartered

Crema or sour cream for serving

Crumbled *cotija* or freshly grated Parmesan cheese for serving

Chile powder for serving

Salt

MAKES 6 SERVINGS

1 Carefully pull the husks back from each ear of corn, remove the silk, and pull the husks back in place. Soak the ears in cold water to cover for about 30 minutes.

2 Prepare a gas or charcoal grill for direct grilling over high heat (page 293). Oil the grill rack. Remove the corn from the water and place directly over the heat elements or over the hottest part of the fire. Grill, turning frequently, until the corn is tender, about 20 minutes. If the husk is very burned but the corn is not yet tender, wrap in aluminum foil and continue grilling until done.

3 Carefully pull back the husks and tie them in place with strips of husk. Rub the corn with the lime quarters, drizzle with some of the *crema,* and sprinkle with the cheese, chile powder, and salt. Transfer to a platter and serve at once. Alternatively, let diners shuck their own corn. Put the limes, *crema*, and cheese in separate small bowls. Place the chile powder and salt in shakers or small bowls. Diners can dress the corn with toppings as they like.

Refried Black Beans

½ cup (4 fl oz/125 ml) canola oil, plus extra if needed

½ white onion, finely chopped

4 cups (28 oz/875 g) cooked black beans, homemade (page 287) or canned, with their liquid

Salt

⅔ cup (3 oz/90 g) crumbled *queso fresco* or feta cheese for serving (optional)

MAKES 4–6 SERVINGS

1 In a large, heavy frying pan over medium heat, warm the oil. Add the onion and sauté, stirring frequently, until soft and golden, about 5 minutes.

2 Slowly and in stages, add the beans with their liquid, smashing the beans with the back of a large wooden spoon. Continue until all of the beans and their liquid have been mashed to a coarse purée. Raise the heat to medium-high and cook, stirring occasionally, until the purée begins to dry out, about 10 minutes, adding more oil if needed. Season with salt.

3 Transfer the beans to a serving bowl and garnish with the cheese, if desired. Serve at once.

These homey beans are a great side dish for many of the recipes in this chapter. They are also delicious served with tortilla chips.

Spicy Sweet Potatoes

2 lb (1 kg) orange-fleshed sweet
potatoes, peeled and cut into
1½-inch (4-cm) chunks

2 tbsp canola oil

Salt

1 tbsp dark brown sugar

1 tbsp finely chopped chipotle
chiles in adobo sauce

1 tsp *each* orange juice
and lemon juice

¼ cup (⅓ oz/10 g) minced
fresh cilantro

½ cup (4 oz/125 g)
sour cream

MAKES 4–6 SERVINGS

1 Preheat the oven to 400°F (200°C). In a bowl, combine the sweet potatoes with the oil and 1 tsp salt and toss to coat well. Spread in a single layer on a rimmed baking sheet and bake, without turning, until tender-crisp and lightly browned, 35–40 minutes.

2 Remove the pan from the oven; leave the oven on. Using a thin-bladed spatula, carefully loosen the sweet potatoes from the baking sheet. Sprinkle with the brown sugar and chipotle chiles and turn gently to coat. Spread in a single layer again and bake for 5 minutes longer.

3 Transfer the sweet potatoes to a serving dish and drizzle with the orange and lemon juices. Garnish with the cilantro and serve with sour cream.

In this hearty side dish, the sugary edge of sweet potatoes is balanced by smoky, spicy chipotle chiles, bright citrus, and rich sour cream.

With its flavors of coffee and cinnamon, this rendition of flan, a delicate custard which originated in Spain, feels thoroughly Mexican.

Caramel-Coffee Flan

8 cups (64 fl oz/2 l) whole milk

1²⁄₃ cups (13 oz/410 g) sugar

2-inch (5-cm) piece cinnamon stick

6 eggs, plus 4 egg yolks

2 tbsp Kahlúa or other coffee liqueur

1 tbsp dark rum

1 tsp pure vanilla extract

Boiling water

MAKES 6–8 SERVINGS

1 In a large saucepan over medium-low heat, bring the milk, 1 cup (8 oz/ 250 g) of the sugar, and the cinnamon stick to a boil, stirring to dissolve the sugar. Reduce the heat to low. Simmer uncovered, stirring frequently, until reduced by about half, about 45 minutes. Set aside to cool.

2 Have ready 6–8 ovenproof custard cups or small ramekins. Place the remaining ²⁄₃ cup (5 oz/160 g) sugar and ¼ cup (2 fl oz/60 ml) water in a small, heavy saucepan over medium-high heat and bring to a boil. Continue to boil without stirring until the syrup begins to color, about 15 minutes. Reduce the heat to a simmer, then swirl the pan until the syrup is a deep amber, about 1 minute. Immediately pour the caramel into the custard cups, dividing it evenly and tilting to distribute the caramel in each cup. Set aside.

3 Preheat the oven to 350°F (180°C). In a large bowl, beat the eggs, egg yolks, Kahlúa, rum, and vanilla until blended. Slowly beat in the milk mixture. Pour the mixture through a fine-mesh sieve into the prepared cups. Place the cups in a baking pan large enough to hold them in a single layer and pour in boiling water to reach three-fourths up the sides of the cups. Cover the baking pan loosely with aluminum foil. Bake until the flans are just set and the tip of a knife inserted in the middle comes out clean, 30–40 minutes. Remove the baking pan from the oven and let the flans cool completely in the water. (The flans can be covered and refrigerated at this point for up to 2 days.)

4 Run a knife around the edge of the molds, invert an individual plate over the top, and invert the flan and dish together. If it resists unmolding, dip the mold in hot water for just a few seconds, then invert. The flan should drop out easily. Repeat with the remaining flans, and serve at once.

These rich cookies are often served for special occasions and use what were once the most prized ingredients: nuts, sugar, and butter.

Mexican Wedding Cookies

½ cup (4 oz/125 g) unsalted butter, at room temperature

½ cup (4 oz/125 g) solid vegetable shortening

2½ cups (8 oz/250 g) sifted powdered sugar

1 tsp finely grated orange zest

1 tbsp fresh orange juice

2 cups (10 oz/315 g) flour

⅔ cup (2½ oz/75 g) ground walnuts or pecans

Salt

MAKES ABOUT
3 DOZEN COOKIES

1 In a bowl, using an electric mixer on medium speed, beat together the butter and shortening until creamy. Add 1½ cups (4½ oz/140 g) of the powdered sugar, the orange zest, and orange juice and beat until blended.

2 In another bowl, stir together the flour, walnuts, and ¼ tsp salt. Add the flour mixture 1 tbsp at a time to the butter mixture, beating until thoroughly incorporated. The dough will be crumbly. Transfer the dough to a large sheet of plastic wrap and press it into a ball. Wrap and refrigerate for at least 1 hour.

3 Position a rack in the upper third of the oven and preheat to 325°F (165°C). Line a baking sheet with parchment or with a silicone baking mat. Using your hands, roll small pieces of the dough into ¾-inch (2-cm) balls. Place the balls on the prepared baking sheet, spacing them about 1 inch (2.5 cm) apart and gently pressing them to flatten slightly. Bake the cookies until the edges turn pale gold, 10–15 minutes.

4 Meanwhile, place the remaining 1 cup (3 oz/90 g) powdered sugar in a shallow bowl. When the cookies are ready, remove the baking sheet from the oven. While they are still hot, using a spatula, remove the cookies one at a time and carefully roll them in the sugar. Set aside on a rack and let cool completely, then roll them again in the sugar, shaking off any excess. Serve at once.

Raspberry Agua Fresca

½ cup (3½ oz/105 g)
superfine sugar

1 cup (4 oz/125 g) raspberries

½ cup (½ oz/15 g) loosely
packed fresh mint leaves,
plus 4 sprigs for garnish

Ice cubes for serving

MAKES 4 SERVINGS

1 In a saucepan, combine the sugar and ½ cup (4 fl oz/125 ml) water. Bring to a simmer over medium-low heat, stirring to dissolve the sugar. Remove the sugar syrup from the heat and let cool.

2 Reserve 4 of the raspberries for garnish. In a blender or food processor, combine the remaining raspberries, the mint leaves, and the sugar syrup and process to a smooth purée. Strain the purée through a fine-mesh sieve into a pitcher. You should have about ⅔ cup (5 fl oz/160 ml). Add 1⅓ cups (11 fl oz/ 340 ml) water. Fill 4 glasses with ice and divide the raspberry mixture among the glasses. Garnish each glass with a mint sprig and one of the reserved raspberries. Serve at once.

Aguas frescas are cool, refreshing drinks typically made from seasonal fruits such as berries or mango.

Spicy Hot Cocoa

6 tbsp (1 oz/30 g) unsweetened
cocoa powder

2 tbsp sugar

1 dried red chile

5 cinnamon sticks

2½ cups (20 fl oz/625 ml)
whole milk

Whipped Cream (page 289)
for garnish (optional)

MAKES 4 SERVINGS

1 In a saucepan over low heat, stir together the cocoa powder, sugar, chile, and ⅓ cup (3 fl oz/80 ml) water. Place over low heat and cook, stirring, until the mixture forms a smooth paste, 3–5 minutes.

2 Add 1 of the cinnamon sticks, pour in the milk, and stir until the paste is completely dissolved. Cook until hot, about 5 minutes. Do not allow the milk to boil. Strain the hot cocoa into 4 mugs and garnish each with a cinnamon stick and a dollop of the whipped cream, if desired. Serve at once.

This recipe mimics the original hot cocoa reputedly made by the Aztecs and that is still served today in parts of southern Mexico.

Serve this memorable tart with chocolate sauce, whipped cream, or tropical fruits such as pineapple or papaya.

Coconut Tart

24 shortbread cookies or vanilla or chocolate wafer cookies

¼ cup (2 oz/60 g) sugar

6 tbsp (3 oz/90 g) unsalted butter, melted

1 cup (8 fl oz/250 ml) canned or thawed frozen coconut water (page 295)

1½ cups (6 oz/185 g) sweetened shredded dried coconut

1 cup (8 fl oz/250 ml) sweetened condensed milk

3 eggs plus 1 egg yolk, beaten

2 tsp pure vanilla extract

½ cup (1½ oz/45 g) flaked coconut, toasted (page 290), for garnish

MAKES 8–10 SERVINGS

1 Preheat the oven to 350°F (180°C). Put the cookies in a blender or food processor and pulse until fine crumbs form. You should have about 1½ cups (6 oz/185 g) crumbs.

2 In a bowl, stir together the cookie crumbs and sugar. Add the melted butter and stir until the mixture holds together when pinched. Transfer to an 11-inch (28-cm) tart pan with removable sides. Press the crumbs evenly in the bottom and up the sides of the pan, using your fingers and the bottom of a glass to pack the crumbs firmly. Transfer the pan to a rimmed baking sheet and bake until the crust is golden and lightly puffed on the bottom, about 7 minutes. Remove from the oven and press firmly on the crumbs again with the bottom of the glass while the crust is still hot.

3 Pour the coconut water into a small saucepan. Add the dried coconut, stir to mix well, and bring to a boil over medium-high heat. Reduce the heat to medium-low and simmer for 10 minutes. Remove from the heat and let cool completely. In a large bowl, whisk together the condensed milk, eggs, and egg yolk until blended. Stir in the vanilla and the cooled coconut mixture.

4 Pour the filling into the crust and bake until the top is slightly puffed, the center is set, and a small wooden skewer inserted into the center of the tart comes out clean, about 35 minutes. Transfer to a wire rack and let cool.

5 Scatter the toasted coconut over the tart. Remove the sides from the tart pan and serve at once.

This rich, puddinglike cake—a favorite in Mexico—translates to "three milks" because it is soaked in three types of dairy products.

Tres Leches Cake

½ cup (4 oz/125 g) vegetable shortening, plus extra for greasing

2¼ cups (9 oz/280 g) sifted flour, plus extra for dusting

1½ cups (12 oz/375 g) sugar

2 eggs

2 tsp baking powder

Salt

1 cup (8 fl oz/250 ml) whole milk

2 tsp pure vanilla extract

1 cup (8 fl oz/250 ml) heavy cream

1 can (14 fl oz/430 ml) sweetened condensed milk

1 can (12 fl oz/375 ml) evaporated milk

2 tbsp dark rum

Meringue Frosting (page 289)

MAKES 12 SERVINGS

1 Preheat the oven to 350°F (180°C). Line a 9-by-12-inch (23-by-30-cm) baking pan with aluminum foil and lightly grease and flour the foil.

2 In a bowl, using an electric mixer set on high speed, beat the shortening until fluffy. Add the sugar a little at a time, beating until fluffy between each addition. Reduce the speed to low and add the eggs one at a time, scraping down the sides of the bowl as needed, until fully incorporated, about 2 minutes total.

3 Sift the flour again with the baking powder and ½ tsp salt into a large bowl. In a small bowl, whisk together the whole milk and 1 tsp of the vanilla. Add one-third of the milk mixture to the shortening and beat until well mixed, then add one-third of the flour mixture. Repeat twice more, beating well after each addition. Scrape the batter into the prepared pan and bake until a wooden skewer inserted into the center of the cake comes out clean, about 35 minutes. Transfer to a wire rack and let cool in the pan for 10 minutes, then invert the cake onto a serving platter and let cool completely.

4 Meanwhile, in a large bowl, whisk together the cream, condensed milk, evaporated milk, rum, and the remaining 1 tsp vanilla.

5 When the cake has cooled completely, poke it all over with the tines of a fork and spoon the milk mixture over the surface, a little at a time, allowing the cake to absorb the sauce before adding more. Cover the cake with plastic wrap and refrigerate for about 1 hour.

6 Spread the meringue frosting thickly over the chilled cake, cover, and refrigerate until well chilled, at least 3 hours and up to 8 hours. Serve the cake chilled, cut into squares.

Indian

This popular griddle bread, called *paratha,* is traditionally made with ghee, or clarified butter, a common ingredient in Indian food.

Flaky Whole-Wheat Flatbread

1½ cups (7½ oz/235 g) whole-wheat flour

1½ cups (7½ oz/235 g) all-purpose flour, plus extra for dusting

Salt

¼ cup (2 oz/60 g) ghee (page 295) or ¼ cup (2 fl oz/ 60 ml) canola oil, plus extra for brushing and frying

MAKES 12 FLATBREADS

1 Sift together the whole-wheat flour, the 1½ cups all-purpose flour, and 1 tsp salt into a large bowl. Add the ¼ cup ghee and use your fingers to rub it into the flour mixture until it is the consistency of coarse meal. Slowly drizzle in 1¼ cups (10 fl oz/310 ml) cold water, mixing and pressing with your hands to incorporate, until the mixture comes together in a rough mass. Turn the dough out onto a lightly floured work surface. Knead until smooth and elastic, about 10 minutes, dusting with flour as needed to prevent sticking. Brush the dough with ghee, cover with plastic wrap, and let rest at room temperature for about 30 minutes.

2 On a lightly floured work surface, roll the dough into a cylinder about 18 inches (45 cm) long, and cut it crosswise into 12 equal pieces. Roll each piece into a ball and cover with a damp kitchen towel. Working with 1 dough ball at a time, use a rolling pin to flatten it into a disk and then roll it out into a 6-inch (15-cm) round, dusting often with flour. Brush the dough with ghee and fold the round in half. Brush more ghee over the top and fold the half-circle in half again to form a triangle. Roll out the triangle into a larger triangle with sides about 8 inches (20 cm) long.

3 Preheat the oven to 250°F (120°C). Heat a large, heavy frying pan over high heat until hot. Brush the pan with ghee, place a dough triangle in it, and reduce the heat to medium-high. Cook until the first side is golden brown in spots, about 2 minutes. Turn and cook until golden brown on the other side, about 3 minutes longer. Keep warm in the oven while you cook the remaining breads. Serve at once.

Originally a colonial English adaptation of Indian cuisine, this formerly thin soup has evolved into a thick, rich meal in a bowl.

Mulligatawny Soup

1 cup (7 oz/220 g) red lentils

1 tsp *each* ground cumin and ground coriander

½ tsp ground turmeric

¼ tsp ground cinnamon

⅛ tsp ground cardamom

2 tbsp canola oil

1 yellow onion, chopped

1 tbsp grated fresh ginger

4 cloves garlic, minced

2 tsp seeded and minced jalapeño chiles

6 cups (48 fl oz/1.5 l) chicken stock, homemade (page 283) or purchased

2 carrots, chopped

1 large green apple, peeled, cored, and chopped

1 large boiling potato such as Yukon gold, peeled and chopped

1 tbsp fresh lemon juice

Salt

2 tbsp minced fresh cilantro

MAKES 4–6 SERVINGS

1 Pick over the lentils, removing any stones or misshapen or discolored lentils. Rinse and place in a bowl with warm water to cover. Let the lentils soak for about 30 minutes.

2 In a small bowl, combine the cumin, coriander, turmeric, cinnamon, and cardamom and stir to mix well. Set aside.

3 In a large saucepan over medium-high heat, warm the oil. Add the onion, ginger, garlic, and jalapeños and sauté until fragrant, about 1 minute. Add the spice mixture and cook, stirring, for 1 minute longer. Pour in the stock and bring to a boil. Drain the lentils and add to the stock. Stir in the carrots, apple, and potato and return to a boil. Reduce the heat to low and simmer, uncovered, until the vegetables and lentils are just tender, 25–30 minutes.

4 Stir in the lemon juice and ½ tsp salt. Taste and adjust the seasoning. Working in batches, transfer about 3 cups (24 fl oz/750 ml) of the warm soup to a blender or food processor and process to a smooth purée. Return to the saucepan and reheat gently, stirring; the soup should be fairly thick. Ladle the soup into warmed bowls, garnish with the cilantro, and serve.

In this Afghan-influenced dish, the subtle sweetness from the squash and a creamy yogurt sauce help balance the spicy flavors.

Spicy Squash with Garlic-Yogurt Sauce

¼ cup (2 fl oz/60 ml) canola oil

2½ lb (1.25 kg) acorn squash, halved lengthwise, seeded, and cut into wedges

1-inch (2.5-cm) piece fresh ginger, grated

1 tsp ground coriander

½ tsp *each* ground cinnamon and red pepper flakes

1 can (14½ oz/455 g) tomato sauce

¼ cup (2 oz/60 g) sugar

Salt and freshly ground black pepper

1½ cups (12 oz/375 g) plain yogurt

2 cloves garlic, minced

3 tbsp minced fresh mint, plus extra for garnish

MAKES 6–8 SERVINGS

1 In a Dutch oven or large, heavy pot over medium-high heat, warm the oil. Working in batches if necessary, add the squash and sauté until evenly browned, about 7 minutes. Transfer to a bowl and set aside. Add the ginger, coriander, cinnamon, and red pepper flakes to the pot and sauté until fragrant, about 30 seconds. Stir in the tomato sauce, sugar, ½ tsp salt, and ¼ tsp black pepper and bring to a boil.

2 Add the squash to the pot and stir to combine with the sauce. Partially cover the pot and simmer gently over low heat until the squash is very tender and the sauce is thick, 30–45 minutes.

3 Meanwhile, line a fine-mesh sieve with a double layer of cheesecloth, place the sieve in a bowl, and spoon the yogurt into the sieve. Refrigerate until the excess liquid has drained from the yogurt, 20–30 minutes. Transfer the thickened yogurt to a bowl. Stir in the garlic, 3 tbsp mint, and ½ tsp salt. Cover and refrigerate until ready to serve.

4 Mound the squash and its sauce on a serving platter. Top with the garlic-yogurt sauce, or put the garlic-yogurt sauce in a bowl and serve alongside the squash. Garnish the squash with mint and serve at once.

Spiced Yellow
Lentil Stew

1½ cups (10½ oz/330 g) yellow lentils

1 tsp ground coriander

1 tsp ground cumin

½ tsp ground turmeric

2 fresh hot green chiles such as serrano, minced

1 tomato, seeded and finely chopped

1½ tsp firmly packed golden brown sugar

Salt

2 tbsp canola or peanut oil

1 tsp brown mustard seeds

1 dried red chile

½ tsp minced garlic

¼ cup (⅓ oz/10 g) minced fresh cilantro (optional)

MAKES 6 SERVINGS

1 Pick over the lentils, discarding any stones or misshapen or discolored lentils. Rinse and place in a deep pot. Add the coriander, cumin, turmeric, green chiles, and 5 cups (40 fl oz/1.25 l) water. Bring to a boil over high heat, then reduce the heat to medium-low and cook at a low boil, uncovered, stirring often, until the lentils are very soft, about 50 minutes.

2 When the lentils are soft, beat them with a wooden spoon to make a chunky purée. Add the tomato, brown sugar, and 1 tsp salt and mix until the sugar dissolves. Reduce the heat to very low to keep warm while you make the spice mixture.

3 In a small frying pan over medium-high heat, warm the oil. When hot, add the mustard seeds and cover the pan. When the sputtering stops, after about 30 seconds, uncover and add the dried chile. Continue frying until the chile turns almost black, about 30 seconds longer; using tongs, remove and discard the chile. Add the garlic to the pan, stir briefly, and immediately pour the contents of the pan over the lentils. Mix, ladle into small bowls, and serve at once garnished with the cilantro, if desired.

Eggplant Curry
with Tomatoes

1 large globe eggplant,
about 2 lb (1 kg)

4 tbsp (2 fl oz/60 ml) canola oil

1 small yellow onion, minced

1 tbsp grated fresh ginger

2 cloves garlic, minced

1 tsp ground cumin

½ tsp *each* ground coriander
and ground turmeric

⅛ tsp cayenne pepper

Salt

1 cup (6 oz/185 g)
chopped tomatoes

½ cup (2½ oz/75 g) fresh or
thawed frozen English peas

1 tbsp chopped fresh cilantro

MAKES 4–6 SERVINGS

1 Preheat the oven to 400°F (200°C). Trim the stem from the eggplant and cut in half lengthwise. Using the tip of a sharp knife, score the eggplant flesh lengthwise in several places about 1 inch (2.5 cm) apart and ¼ inch (6 mm) deep. Rub the cut sides with 2 tbsp of the oil.

2 Pour ¼ cup (2 fl oz/60 ml) water into a large rimmed baking sheet. Place the eggplant halves, cut side down, in the prepared pan. Roast until tender when pierced with a fork, about 25 minutes. Transfer to a plate and let cool. Using a large spoon, scoop out the flesh onto a cutting board. Discard the skin. Chop the eggplant flesh.

3 In a large frying pan over medium-high heat, warm the remaining 2 tbsp oil. Add the onion, ginger, and garlic and sauté until the onion is beginning to brown, 4–5 minutes. Stir in the cumin, coriander, turmeric, cayenne, and 1 tsp salt and sauté until the spices are fragrant, about 1 minute.

4 Add the eggplant and tomatoes, reduce the heat to low, and simmer, stirring occasionally, until the curry has thickened, about 10 minutes. Stir in the peas and simmer for 5 minutes longer.

5 Taste and adjust the seasoning. Transfer the curry to a warmed bowl, garnish with the cilantro, and serve at once.

This flavorful yellow curry develops a complex bouquet through slow simmering. Try it with medium-sized shrimp instead of fish.

Spicy Fish Curry

⅓ cup (3 fl oz/80 ml) canola oil

1 yellow onion, finely chopped

2 cloves garlic, minced

2 fresh hot green chiles such as serrano, seeded and minced

1-inch (2.5-cm) piece fresh ginger, grated

1 tbsp ground cumin

2 tsp *each* ground coriander, brown mustard seeds, and ground turmeric

2 tomatoes, cored and chopped

1 tbsp sugar

Salt

2 lb (1 kg) firm, mild white fish fillets such as tilapia, cod, or halibut, cut into chunks

Steamed Rice (page 288) for serving

3 tbsp minced fresh cilantro

MAKES 6–8 SERVINGS

1 In a Dutch oven or large, heavy pot over medium-high heat, warm the oil. Add the onion and sauté until it starts to turn golden, 5–7 minutes. Stir in the garlic, chiles, ginger, cumin, coriander, mustard seeds, and turmeric and sauté until the spices are fragrant and the onion is evenly coated, about 1 minute. Add the tomatoes, sugar, and 1 tsp salt and sauté until the tomatoes begin to release their juices, 4–5 minutes. Pour in 1½ cups (12 fl oz/375 ml) water and deglaze the pot, scraping the bottom with a wooden spoon to dislodge any browned bits. Reduce the heat to low, partially cover the pot, and cook gently for about 15 minutes.

2 Uncover the pot and add the fish, stirring gently to coat it with the sauce. Partially cover the pot again and cook until the fish is opaque throughout and the sauce is thick, about 30 minutes longer. Check the sauce halfway through the cooking time; if it seems to be getting too thick, stir in more water, about ½ cup (4 fl oz/125 ml) at a time. Season to taste with salt.

3 Divide the rice among warmed individual bowls. Top the rice with the curry and garnish each serving with some of the cilantro. Serve at once.

Braised Fish in Coconut

2 tbsp canola oil

1 onion, chopped

3 cloves garlic, minced

½ tsp *each* cayenne pepper, ground coriander, and ground turmeric

¼ tsp *each* ground cumin and fennel seeds

Salt and freshly ground black pepper

Pinch *each* of ground cinnamon and ground cloves

2 tomatoes, cored and chopped

1 can (13½ fl oz/420 ml) coconut milk

1 tbsp tamarind paste dissolved in 3 tbsp warm water (optional)

1 tsp sugar

2 lb (1 kg) halibut, salmon, or sea bass fillets, cut into serving pieces

MAKES 6–8 SERVINGS

1 In a large, wide saucepan over medium heat, warm the oil. Add the onion and garlic and sauté until just barely tender, about 3 minutes. Add the cayenne, coriander, turmeric, cumin, fennel seeds, ¼ tsp black pepper, cinnamon, and cloves and sauté until the spices are fragrant and evenly coat the onion and garlic, about 30 seconds. Add the tomatoes and sauté until they release their juices, about 1 minute. Stir in the coconut milk, dissolved tamarind paste (if using), sugar, and ¾ tsp salt. Bring to a boil and deglaze the pan, scraping the bottom with a wooden spoon to dislodge any browned bits. Partially cover the pan and cook over low heat for 25 minutes.

2 Uncover the pan and add the fish, then partially cover and cook until the fish is flaky but still very moist and the sauce is thickened, about 20 minutes longer. Transfer the fish and sauce to warmed plates and serve at once.

Gentle braising makes this fish melt-in-your-mouth tender in this mildly-spiced dish flavored with coconut.

Tandoori-Style Fish

½ cup (4 oz/125 g) plain yogurt

1 tbsp fresh lemon juice

1 shallot, chopped

3 cloves garlic, chopped

1 tbsp chopped fresh ginger

1 jalapeño chile, seeded and chopped

2 tsp garam masala

1 tsp ground turmeric

Salt

4 sea bass or halibut fillets, each about 6 oz (185 g)

2 tbsp canola oil, plus extra for brushing

1 large yellow onion, thinly sliced

3 sprigs fresh cilantro

1 lemon, cut into wedges

MAKES 4 SERVINGS

1 To make the marinade, in a blender or food processor, combine the yogurt, lemon juice, shallot, garlic, ginger, jalapeño, garam masala, turmeric, and 1 tsp salt and process to a smooth purée.

2 Pour the marinade into a large zippered plastic bag. Add the fish fillets to the marinade, seal the bag, and massage to coat the fillets with the mixture. Refrigerate for at least 1 hour or up to 2 hours.

3 In a large frying pan over medium heat, warm the oil. Add the onion and sauté until soft and golden brown, 10–12 minutes. Remove from the heat and cover to keep warm.

4 Prepare a gas or charcoal grill for direct grilling over high heat (page 293), or preheat the broiler. Oil the grill rack or broiler pan. Remove the fish fillets from the marinade. Shake off the excess marinade and discard. Place the fish directly over the heat elements or over the hottest part of the fire; if using a broiler, position the pan 4–6 inches (10–15 cm) from the heat source. Cook until the fish is golden brown on the first side, 4–5 minutes. Using a spatula, carefully turn the fillets and cook until golden brown on the other side, about 4 minutes longer. Move the fish to a cooler area of the grill and cover the grill, or turn off the broiler, and let the fillets continue to cook until opaque throughout, about 5 minutes.

5 Gently reheat the onions in the frying pan and mound three-fourths of them on a warmed platter. Arrange the fillets on top. Garnish with the remaining onions, the cilantro sprigs, and the lemon wedges. Serve at once.

One of the richest yet mildest curries, this Indian dish is beloved for its creamy sauce. Here, it is lightened with buttermilk.

Chicken Korma

¼ cup (2 fl oz/60 ml) canola oil

1 yellow onion, finely chopped

2 cloves garlic, minced

2-inch (5-cm) piece fresh ginger, grated

2-inch (5-cm) cinnamon stick

2 bay leaves

1 tbsp *each* ground coriander and ground turmeric

½ tsp *each* cayenne pepper and ground cumin

1½ cups (12 fl oz/375 ml) chicken stock, homemade (page 283) or purchased

1 cup (8 fl oz/250 ml) canned tomato sauce

1 tbsp sugar

Salt

2 lb (1 kg) skinless, boneless chicken breasts, cut into strips

½ cup (4 fl oz/125 ml) buttermilk

½ cup (3 oz/90 g) unsalted roasted cashews

Steamed Rice (page 288) for serving

3 tbsp chopped fresh cilantro

MAKES 6–8 SERVINGS

1 In a Dutch oven or large, heavy pot over medium-high heat, warm the oil. Add the onion and sauté until it begins to soften, about 3 minutes. Add the garlic, ginger, cinnamon stick, bay leaves, coriander, turmeric, cayenne, and cumin and sauté until the spices are fragrant and evenly coat the onion, about 1 minute. Stir in the stock, tomato sauce, sugar, and 1 tsp salt, bring to a boil, and deglaze the pot, scraping the bottom with a wooden spoon to dislodge any browned bits.

2 Add the chicken strips to the pot and stir to coat evenly. Partially cover the pot and cook over low heat until the chicken is very tender and the sauce is thickened, about 1 hour.

3 About 15 minutes before the chicken is done, combine the buttermilk and cashews in a blender or food processor and process until the nuts are finely puréed and combined with the buttermilk. Add the nut mixture to the chicken mixture and stir to blend with the sauce. Continue cooking until the sauce is completely heated through and thick, about 5 minutes. Remove and discard the bay leaves and cinnamon stick.

4 Divide the rice among warmed bowls. Top with the chicken and sauce and garnish with the cilantro. Serve at once.

Chicken Tikka Masala

1½ lb (750 g) skinless, boneless chicken breasts, cut into cubes

Indian Yogurt Marinade (page 287)

2 tbsp canola oil, plus extra as needed

1 yellow onion, chopped

2 tbsp grated fresh ginger

2 cloves garlic, chopped

1 red Fresno chile, chopped

¼ tsp *each* sugar and garam masala

Pinch of cayenne pepper

1 cup (8 fl oz/250 ml) *each* tomato purée and chicken stock, homemade (page 283) or purchased

¼ cup (2 oz/60 g) plain yogurt

½ cup (4 fl oz/125 ml) half-and-half

1 tbsp chopped fresh cilantro

MAKES 4–6 SERVINGS

1 Add the chicken to the marinade and stir to coat thoroughly. Cover and refrigerate for at least 4 hours or up to overnight. Soak 10 long bamboo skewers in cold water to cover for at least 30 minutes.

2 Prepare a gas or charcoal grill for direct grilling over high heat (page 293). Remove the chicken from the marinade and pat dry with paper towels. Discard the marinade. Thread the chicken onto the skewers. Brush the chicken and the grill rack with oil. Place the skewers directly over the heat elements or over the hottest part of the fire and sear until golden brown on both sides, turning once, 7–9 minutes. Transfer to a platter and set aside.

3 In a blender or food processor, process the onion, ginger, garlic, chile, and 2 tbsp water until a smooth paste forms. In a large frying pan over medium-high heat, warm the 2 tbsp oil. Add the onion paste and sauté until it begins to brown, about 5 minutes. Stir in the sugar, garam masala, and cayenne and sauté for 1 minute. Add the tomato purée and stock, reduce the heat to medium-low, and bring to a simmer. Cook, stirring often, until the sauce thickens, 5–6 minutes. Reduce the heat to low and stir in the yogurt and half- and-half. Bring to a simmer and cook for 5 minutes to blend the flavors.

4 Slide the chicken pieces off the skewers into the sauce and stir to combine. Cook until the chicken is opaque throughout, about 5 minutes longer. Taste and adjust the seasoning. Transfer to a warmed bowl, garnish with the cilantro, and serve at once.

Tandoori-Style Chicken

8 whole bone-in chicken
legs, skinned

Salt

5 tbsp (3 fl oz/80 ml)
fresh lemon juice

Tandoori Marinade (page 287)

2 tbsp unsalted butter or
ghee (page 295), melted

MAKES 6–8 SERVINGS

1 Pat the chicken legs dry with paper towels. Using a sharp knife, cut 2 or 3 slashes in each thigh, about ¾ inch (2 cm) apart, cutting all the way to the bone. Cut 1 slash in the meaty part of each drumstick. Season the chicken with 1 tsp salt, rubbing some of the salt into the slashes with your fingers. Sprinkle with 3 tbsp of the lemon juice, also rubbing some into the slashes.

2 Place the chicken in a nonreactive baking dish, pour the marinade over the chicken, and turn to coat. Cover and refrigerate for at least 12 hours or up to 24 hours, turning the chicken legs occasionally.

3 About 30 minutes prior to roasting, remove the chicken from the refrigerator and wipe off most of the marinade with paper towels. Discard the marinade. Preheat the oven to 450°F (230°C). Line a rimmed baking sheet with heavy-duty aluminum foil. Oil 1 or 2 flat roasting racks and place them in the prepared pan. Place the chicken legs, not touching, on the rack(s).

4 Roast the chicken, without turning, until an instant-read meat thermometer inserted into the thickest part of the thigh away from the bone registers 170°–175°F (77°–80°C), about 25 minutes.

5 Meanwhile, in a bowl, stir together the melted butter and the remaining 2 tbsp lemon juice. When the chicken is ready, remove it from the oven and immediately baste it with the butter–lemon juice mixture. Transfer the chicken legs to a platter. Serve hot, warm, or at room temperature.

Sweet and earthy spices impart rich color and alluring flavor to this elaborate rice dish, which is fit for a celebratory feast.

Chicken Biryani

1 tsp *each* ground cumin, coriander, and turmeric

½ tsp ground cinnamon

¼ tsp *each* ground cardamom and grated nutmeg

⅛ tsp cayenne pepper

4 star anise pods

3 bay leaves

3 yellow onions

4 tbsp (2 fl oz/60 ml) canola oil

1 jalapeño chile

5 cloves garlic, chopped

2 tbsp chopped fresh ginger

1 lb (500 g) skinless, boneless chicken thighs, diced

Salt

½ cup (4 oz/125 g) plain yogurt

3 tbsp fresh lemon juice

1½ cups (10½ oz/330 g) basmati rice

2 hard-boiled eggs (page 292)

¼ cup (1½ oz/45 g) cashews, toasted (page 290) and chopped

¼ cup (⅓ oz/10 g) minced fresh cilantro

¼ cup (1½ oz/45 g) golden raisins

MAKES 6 SERVINGS

1 In a small bowl, stir together the cumin, coriander, turmeric, cinnamon, cardamom, nutmeg, cayenne, star anise, and bay leaves. Set aside. Thinly slice 2 of the onions and chop the third.

2 In a Dutch oven or large ovenproof frying pan over medium heat, warm 2 tbsp of the oil. Add the sliced onions to the pot and cook, stirring often, until golden brown and caramelized, 15–20 minutes. Transfer to a bowl.

3 Meanwhile, seed and chop the jalapeño. In a mini food processor, process the chopped onion, garlic, ginger, and jalapeño until a thick paste forms.

4 Heat 1 tbsp of the oil in the Dutch oven over high heat. Sprinkle the chicken with ¼ tsp salt and arrange in the pot in a single layer. Sear, turning as needed, until golden brown on all sides, about 5 minutes. Transfer to a bowl.

5 Return the Dutch oven to medium heat and warm the remaining 1 tbsp oil. Add the onion-garlic paste and sauté until golden brown, about 5 minutes. Add the spice mixture and sauté until fragrant, about 1 minute. Add the caramelized sliced onions, reserving about ⅓ cup (2 oz/60 g) for garnish. Stir in the yogurt, lemon juice, and ¼ cup (2 fl oz/60 ml) water. Reduce the heat to low, add the seared chicken, and simmer for 2 minutes.

6 Preheat the oven to 350°F (180°C). Add the rice to the simmering liquid in the pot and stir until well coated. Pour in 2 cups (16 fl oz/500 ml) water, raise the heat to medium, and bring to a boil. Cover the pot and transfer to the oven. Bake for 30 minutes. Remove from the oven and let rest, covered, for 10 minutes. Meanwhile, peel the hard-boiled eggs and cut into wedges.

7 Fluff the rice with a fork and transfer the chicken and rice to a warmed serving dish or platter. Garnish with the reserved caramelized onions, egg wedges, cashews, cilantro, and golden raisins. Serve at once.

Although this well-balanced stew is not overwhelmingly hot, it is delicious served with creamy, cooling Raita (page 286).

Pork Vindaloo

2½–3 lb (1.25–1.5 kg) boneless pork shoulder, trimmed of excess fat and cut into cubes

Salt and freshly ground black pepper

½ cup (4 fl oz/125 ml) canola oil

2 yellow onions, finely chopped

8 cloves garlic, minced

2-inch (5-cm) piece fresh ginger, grated

1½ tsp *each* cayenne pepper, brown mustard seeds, ground cumin, hot paprika, and ground turmeric

½ tsp ground cinnamon

Pinch of ground cloves

⅓ cup (3 fl oz/80 ml) white wine vinegar

1 cup (8 fl oz/250 ml) chicken stock, homemade (page 283) or purchased

Steamed Rice (page 288) for serving

MAKES 6–8 SERVINGS

1 Place the pork in a bowl with 1 tsp each salt and black pepper, and toss to coat evenly. In a Dutch oven or large, heavy pot over medium-high heat, warm the oil. Working in batches, add the pork and cook until browned on all sides, 6–7 minutes. Remove from the pot with a slotted spoon and set aside.

2 Add the onions to the pot, raise the heat to high, and sauté until browned, 10–12 minutes. Add the garlic, ginger, cayenne, mustard seeds, cumin, paprika, turmeric, cinnamon, and cloves and sauté until the spices are fragrant and evenly coat the onion, about 1 minute. Pour in the vinegar and deglaze the pot, scraping the bottom with a wooden spoon to dislodge any browned bits. Stir in the stock and bring to a boil.

3 Add the pork and any accumulated juices to the Dutch oven, partially cover, and cook over low heat until the pork is very tender and the sauce has thickened, 1½–2 hours. To serve, divide the rice among warmed individual plates and top with the pork and sauce.

Serve this hearty curry—not too spicy but packed with flavor—with plenty of fragrant basmati rice to soak up the sauce.

Lamb & Spinach Curry

3 lb (1.5 kg) boneless leg of lamb, cut into cubes

Salt and freshly ground pepper

½ cup (4 fl oz/125 ml) canola oil

2 yellow onions, finely chopped

4 cloves garlic, minced

3 small fresh hot green chiles, seeded and minced

1-inch (2.5-cm) piece fresh ginger, grated

1 tbsp *each* brown mustard seeds, ground cumin, and ground coriander

1½ tsp ground cardamom

1 tsp ground turmeric

1½ cups (12 fl oz/375 ml) chicken stock, homemade (page 283) or purchased

6 cups (6 oz/185 g) baby spinach leaves

1 tbsp garam masala

Steamed Rice (page 288) for serving

1 cup (8 oz/250 g) plain yogurt

MAKES 6–8 SERVINGS

1 Put the lamb in a large bowl with 1 tsp salt and ½ tsp pepper and toss to coat evenly. In a Dutch oven or large, heavy pot over medium-high heat, warm the oil. Working in batches as needed, cook the lamb, turning frequently, until evenly browned on all sides, about 5 minutes. Using a slotted spoon, transfer the lamb to a plate and set aside.

2 Add the onions to the pot and sauté over medium-high heat until golden brown, 7–10 minutes. Add the garlic, chiles, ginger, mustard seeds, cumin, coriander, cardamom, and turmeric and stir until the spices are fragrant and evenly coat the onions, about 1 minute. Pour in the stock and deglaze the pot, scraping the bottom with a wooden spoon to dislodge any browned bits. Bring to a boil.

3 Add the reserved lamb and any accumulated juices to the pot. Cover and cook over very low heat until the lamb is very tender, about 3 hours.

4 Meanwhile, bring a large saucepan three-fourths full of water to a boil. Fill a large bowl with ice water. Working in batches, immerse the spinach leaves in the boiling water. As soon as the leaves have wilted completely, after about 30 seconds, use the slotted spoon to transfer them to the bowl of ice water. Squeeze all the water from the spinach, finely chop, and set aside.

5 Add the chopped spinach and garam masala to the lamb and stir to combine. Divide the rice among warmed shallow bowls, top with the lamb curry and garnish with the yogurt. Serve at once.

Mango-Yogurt Lassi

2 ripe mangoes

2½ cups (20 oz/625 g)
plain yogurt

1 tsp fresh lemon juice

¼ cup (2 oz/60 g) sugar,
plus extra as needed

¼ tsp ground cardamom

Salt

1½ cups (12 oz/375 g)
crushed ice

MAKES 4 SERVINGS

1 Stand each mango on a narrow side on a cutting board. Insert the tip of a knife to locate the wide, flat pit. Positioning the knife slightly off center, cut the flesh from one flat side of the pit in a single piece, then cut the flesh from the other side. Score the mango halves in a crosshatch pattern, then turn each half inside out. Trim the flesh from the skin. Trim any excess flesh from the pit.

2 Place the mango flesh, yogurt, lemon juice, sugar, cardamom, and a pinch of salt in a blender. Add the ice and purée until smooth, 30–60 seconds. Taste and adjust the flavor with sugar. Pour into 4 tall glasses and serve.

Similar in consistency to a milk shake, this yogurt drink gains rich flavor from fresh, ripe mangoes. It's the perfect counterpoint to spicy food.

Ice Cream with Pistachios

8 cardamom pods

3 cups (24 fl oz/750 ml)
heavy cream

3 cups (24 fl oz/750 ml)
whole milk

½ cup (4 oz/125 g) sugar

Salt

1 tsp rose water (optional)

3 tbsp chopped
blanched almonds

3 tbsp chopped unsalted
roasted pistachios

MAKES 1 QT (32 FL OZ/1 L)

1 Gently crack each cardamom pod with the side of a chef's knife. In a large saucepan over medium heat, combine the cream and milk and bring almost to a boil, 2–3 minutes. Reduce the heat to low, add the cardamom pods, and simmer, stirring occasionally to prevent a skin from forming, until the mixture is reduced by half, 45–50 minutes.

2 Pour the milk mixture through a fine-mesh sieve into a large bowl and discard the cardamom pods. Return the mixture to the same saucepan, add the sugar and ⅛ tsp salt, and simmer over low heat, stirring, until the sugar is dissolved, about 2 minutes. Return the mixture to the large bowl and stir in the rose water (if using), almonds, and 2 tbsp of the pistachios.

3 Place the bowl in a larger bowl partially filled with ice cubes and stir the mixture while it cools, 10–15 minutes. Pour the mixture into a freezer-proof container, cover with plastic wrap, and freeze overnight.

4 Let the ice cream stand for a few minutes before serving in individual bowls. Garnish with the remaining pistachios.

Infused with cardamom and rose water, this Indian-style ice cream, or *kulfi,* should be served a little soft.

Chinese

Filled with pork and shrimp, the delicate dumplings in this familiar soup go together quickly after a little practice.

Wonton Soup

4 green onions

2 oz (60 g) shrimp, peeled and deveined (page 292), then coarsely chopped

3 oz (90 g) canned water chestnuts, drained and minced

1/4 lb (125 g) ground pork

1 tbsp grated fresh ginger

1 clove garlic, minced

1 egg, lightly beaten

3 tbsp soy sauce

2 tbsp Chinese rice wine

1 tbsp plus 1/2 tsp sesame oil

1 tbsp cornstarch, plus extra for dusting

1/2 tsp sugar

Salt and ground white pepper

6 cups (48 fl oz/1.5 l) chicken stock, homemade (page 283) or purchased

1 tsp ginger juice (page 292) or finely grated fresh ginger

30 square wonton wrappers

MAKES 4–6 SERVINGS

1 Mince 3 of the green onions. In a large bowl, combine the minced green onions, shrimp, water chestnuts, pork, ginger, garlic, egg, 1 tbsp of the soy sauce, 1 tbsp of the rice wine, the 1 tbsp sesame oil, the cornstarch, sugar, 1/8 tsp white pepper, and 1 tbsp water. Using a rubber spatula, stir vigorously until the ingredients are well combined. Refrigerate the filling for 30 minutes.

2 In a large saucepan over medium heat, combine the stock, the remaining 2 tbsp soy sauce, 1 tbsp rice wine, and 1/2 tsp sesame oil, the ginger juice, and 1/2 tsp salt and bring the soup to a gentle boil. Remove from the heat, cover, and set aside.

3 To assemble the wontons, working with one wrapper at a time, place the wrapper on a work surface and moisten the edges with cold water; keep the other wrappers covered with a damp kitchen towel to prevent them from drying out. Place 1 tsp of the filling in the center of the wrapper and fold over into a triangle. Press the edges together firmly to seal. Fold the 2 outer points across the top of the mound and pinch the corners together to seal. If they do not stick, moisten with a little water. Place the finished wontons on a baking sheet dusted with cornstarch.

4 Reheat the soup over low heat. Bring a large pot three-fourths full of salted water to a boil over high heat. Add the wontons to the boiling water, reduce the heat to medium, and simmer gently until they rise to the surface and the wrappers are tender, about 6 minutes. Meanwhile, thinly shred or slice the remaining green onion.

5 Using a slotted spoon or wire skimmer, carefully lift out the wontons and divide among warmed bowls. Ladle the hot soup over the wontons and garnish with the shredded green onion. Serve at once.

This spicy soup gains smoky sweetness from black vinegar, which is available from Asian groceries or online sources.

Hot & Sour Soup

2 oz (60 g) skinless, boneless chicken breast

2 oz (60 g) beef sirloin

½ cup (2 oz/60 g) bamboo shoots

2 oz (60 g) firm tofu

5 oz (155 g) fresh shiitake mushrooms, stemmed and thinly sliced

2 tbsp canola oil

4 green onions, thinly sliced on the diagonal

1 tbsp minced fresh ginger

8 cups (64 fl oz/2 l) chicken stock, homemade (page 283) or purchased

⅓ cup (3 fl oz/80 ml) black vinegar or balsamic vinegar

2 tbsp *each* Chinese rice wine and chile bean paste

1 tbsp soy sauce

2 tsp sesame oil

Ground white pepper

¼ cup (1½ oz/45 g) fresh or thawed frozen English peas

2 tbsp shredded smoked ham

2 eggs, lightly beaten

1 tbsp cornstarch

MAKES 6 SERVINGS

1 Bring a large saucepan three-fourths full of water to a boil over high heat. Cut the chicken, beef, bamboo shoots, and tofu into strips 4 inches (10 cm) long by ¼ inch (6 mm) wide. Add the chicken, beef, bamboo shoots, tofu, and mushrooms to the saucepan and return the water to a boil. Cook for 3 minutes, then drain in a colander and set aside.

2 Add the oil to the saucepan and warm over medium-high heat. Add the green onions and ginger and sauté until fragrant, about 1 minute. Pour in the stock and add the vinegar, rice wine, chile bean paste, soy sauce, sesame oil, and ¼ tsp white pepper. Bring to a boil and cook for 1 minute. Stir in the cooked drained chicken, beef, bamboo shoots, tofu, and mushrooms. Reduce the heat to low and simmer, uncovered, until the chicken and beef are cooked through and the flavors are blended, about 10 minutes. Add the peas and the shredded ham, and stir to combine.

3 Pour the eggs into the soup in a thin, steady stream. Let stand for about 20 seconds to allow the eggs to set in fine strands, then swirl them into the soup. In a small bowl, whisk the cornstarch with 3 tbsp water. Slowly pour about half of the cornstarch mixture into the soup while stirring constantly. The soup will thicken slightly. Add more of the cornstarch mixture as desired, stirring constantly, for a thicker consistency. Ladle the soup into warmed individual bowls and serve at once.

Salt & Pepper Shrimp

2 egg whites

2 tbsp cornstarch

Salt, ground white pepper, and coarsely ground black pepper

2 green onions, minced

2 tbsp minced fresh ginger

3 cloves garlic, minced

1 red Fresno chile, seeded and minced

1 tsp five-spice powder

¼ tsp sugar

2 tbsp canola oil, plus extra for deep-frying

1½ lb (750 g) large shrimp, peeled and deveined (page 292), with tail segments intact

1 tbsp Chinese rice wine

MAKES 4–6 SERVINGS

1 In a bowl, whisk together the egg whites, cornstarch, ½ tsp salt, and 1 tsp white pepper until smooth. Set the mixture aside.

2 In a small bowl, combine the green onions, ginger, garlic, and chile and stir to mix well. In another small bowl, stir together the five-spice powder, the sugar, ½ tsp salt, and ¼ tsp black pepper. Set both mixtures aside.

3 Pour oil to a depth of 3 inches (7.5 cm) into a wok or deep saucepan and heat to 370°F (188°C) on a deep-frying thermometer. Using tongs, dip a shrimp into the egg white mixture, allowing the excess to fall back into the bowl. Slide the shrimp into the hot oil. Repeat to add 4 or 5 more shrimp to the oil, being careful not to crowd the pan. Deep-fry until the crust is light golden brown and the shrimp just turns pink, about 30 seconds. Using a wire skimmer, transfer to paper towels to drain. Repeat to fry the remaining shrimp, allowing the oil to return to 370°F and removing any browned bits of batter from the oil between batches. Remove the used oil from the pan.

4 In the wok or a large frying pan, warm the 2 tbsp oil. When the oil is hot, add the green onion mixture and sauté until fragrant, about 10 seconds. While tossing and stirring constantly, add the five-spice mixture. Sprinkle the rice wine into the pan and stir-fry for just a few seconds, scraping up any browned bits from the bottom of the pan. Return the fried shrimp to the pan and stir-fry until well coated with the spice mixture and heated through. Transfer the fried shrimp to a warmed platter and serve at once.

Cashew Chicken

3 tbsp soy sauce

1 tbsp Chinese rice wine
or dry sherry

2 tsp grated fresh ginger

1 lb (500 g) skinless, boneless
chicken thighs, cut into
bite-sized pieces

1 tsp Worcestershire sauce

1 tsp sesame oil

½ tsp sugar

¼ tsp cornstarch

3 tbsp canola or peanut oil

2 green onions, chopped

1 cup (5½ oz/170 g) salted
roasted cashews

Steamed Rice (page 288)
for serving

MAKES 4 SERVINGS

1 In a large bowl, stir together 2 tbsp of the soy sauce, the rice wine, and the ginger. Add the chicken, stir to coat evenly, and set aside for 15 minutes.

2 In a small bowl, whisk together 2 tbsp water, the remaining 1 tbsp soy sauce, the Worcestershire sauce, sesame oil, sugar, and cornstarch to make a stir-fry sauce. Set aside.

3 Heat a wok or large frying pan over high heat until very hot and add 2 tbsp of the oil. Remove the chicken from the marinade, draining it well, and discard the marinade. Add the chicken to the pan and stir-fry until opaque, about 3 minutes. Using a slotted spoon, transfer the chicken to a bowl. Return the pan to medium heat and add the remaining 1 tbsp oil. Add the green onions and stir-fry until wilted and fragrant, about 10 seconds. Return the chicken to the pan and add the cashews. Give the sauce a quick stir, add it to the pan, and stir until the sauce thickens slightly, 1–2 minutes. Serve at once over the rice.

This easy-to-make, popular dish uses ingredients that you're likely to have on hand in your pantry.

Sweet and savory spices enhance the rich flavor and texture of slowly braised duck breasts in this memorable dish.

Allspice Duck with Braised Bok Choy

3 tbsp canola oil

4 lb (2 kg) boneless duck breasts, trimmed of excess skin and fat

Salt and freshly ground pepper

2 yellow onions, finely chopped

2 cloves garlic, minced

1-inch (2.5-cm) piece fresh ginger, grated

1½ tbsp ground allspice

1 cinnamon stick

1 star anise pod, broken into pieces

1½ cups (12 fl oz/375 ml) chicken stock, homemade (page 283) or purchased

¼ cup (2 oz/60 g) firmly packed dark brown sugar

¼ cup (2 fl oz/60 ml) soy sauce

3 tbsp hoisin sauce

6 baby bok choy, about 2 lb (1 kg) total weight, each quartered lengthwise

MAKES 6–8 SERVINGS

1 In a Dutch oven or large, heavy pot over medium-high heat, warm the oil. Season the duck breasts generously with salt and pepper. Place in the pot, skin side down, and cook until well browned on both sides, turning once, about 10 minutes. Remove from the pot and set aside.

2 Pour off all but a thin coating of fat in the pot. Add the onions, garlic, ginger, allspice, cinnamon stick, and star anise and sauté over medium-high heat until the onions begin to soften, about 3 minutes. Add the stock and deglaze the pot, scraping up the bottom with a wooden spoon to dislodge any browned bits. Stir in the sugar, soy sauce, and hoisin and bring to a boil.

3 Add the duck breasts back to the pot. Partially cover and cook over very low heat for 1 hour. Uncover, and, using a spoon, skim off the fat from the surface of the pan juices. Arrange the bok choy quarters around the duck breasts, pushing them slightly into the cooking liquid. Partially cover and cook until the duck is very tender and the sauce is thick, 30 minutes longer.

4 Remove the duck breasts and slice them against the grain, on the diagonal. Arrange the slices on warmed plates with the bok choy and spoon the sauce over the top. Serve at once.

Braised Pork Spareribs

2 tbsp oyster sauce

3 tbsp soy sauce

2 tbsp Chinese rice wine

2 tbsp fermented black beans, rinsed well and drained

1 tsp sugar

2 tsp sesame oil

Salt and ground white pepper

5 green onions

1 tbsp cornstarch

2½ lb (1.25 kg) pork spareribs, cut crosswise into 2-inch (5-cm) pieces by the butcher

5 tbsp (3 fl oz/80 ml) canola oil

3 cloves garlic, minced

1 tbsp minced fresh ginger

2 red Fresno chiles, 1 seeded and minced, 1 cut into thin rings

MAKES 4–6 SERVINGS

1 In a bowl, combine the oyster sauce, soy sauce, rice wine, black beans, sugar, sesame oil, and ⅛ tsp white pepper. Add 3 cups (24 fl oz/750 ml) water and mix well. Set aside. Shred 1 green onion and set aside.

2 In a small bowl, whisk together the cornstarch and ½ tsp salt. Sprinkle the cornstarch mixture evenly over the sparerib pieces. In a Dutch oven or large, heavy pot over high heat, warm 2 tbsp of the canola oil. When the oil is hot, add half of the spareribs in a single layer and sear, turning once, until crisp and golden brown on both sides, 8–10 minutes total. Transfer the seared ribs to a bowl. Add 2 tbsp of the oil to the pot and repeat to sear the second batch of spareribs.

3 Preheat the oven to 325°F (165°C). Mince the remaining 4 green onions. Place the same pot over medium-high heat and warm the remaining 1 tbsp oil. Add the minced green onion, garlic, ginger, and minced chile. Sauté until the onions and garlic are tender and translucent, about 3 minutes. Add the soy sauce mixture and bring to a boil. Reduce the heat to low. Return the ribs and any accumulated juices to the pot and stir gently. Cover the pot tightly and place in the oven. Bake until the meat is very tender and almost falling off the bone, 1½–2 hours. Stir the ribs 2 or 3 times during the braising.

4 Transfer the spareribs and sauce to a warmed serving bowl or platter, garnish with the shredded green onion and chile rings, and serve at once.

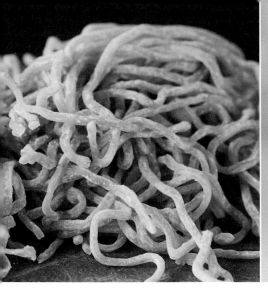

Shanghai Pork Noodles

1 lb (500 g) fresh Chinese egg noodles

5 tbsp (3 fl oz/80 ml) canola or peanut oil

¼ cup (2 fl oz/60 ml) soy sauce

3 tbsp Worcestershire sauce

2 tbsp rice vinegar

1 tsp sugar

Ground white pepper

½ lb (250 g) boneless pork loin, cut across the grain into thin strips

1 yellow onion, thinly sliced

2 red bell peppers, seeded and thinly sliced crosswise

2 cloves garlic, minced

½ head napa cabbage, finely shredded

MAKES 4 SERVINGS

1 Bring a large pot of water to a boil. Separate the strands of noodles, drop them into the boiling water, and boil for 2 minutes. Drain and rinse with running cold water. Place in a bowl, add 1 tbsp of the oil, and toss to coat.

2 In a small bowl, stir together ⅓ cup (3 fl oz/80 ml) warm water and the soy sauce, Worcestershire sauce, vinegar, sugar, and a pinch of white pepper.

3 Heat a wok or large frying pan over high heat until very hot and add 2 tbsp of the oil. Add the pork and stir-fry just until browned, 3 minutes. Using a slotted spoon, transfer the pork to a bowl. Return the pan to high heat and add the remaining 2 tbsp oil. Add the onion and bell peppers and stir-fry just until tender, 5 minutes. Stir in the garlic and cabbage and stir-fry until the cabbage begins to wilt, 3 minutes. Pour in the sauce and bring to a boil. Stir in the noodles and pork and mix well with the vegetables. Cover, reduce the heat to low, and cook, stirring once or twice, until the noodles have absorbed the sauce, about 10 minutes. Transfer to bowls and serve at once.

Tender pork, sweet peppers, and crisp cabbage make a quick stir-fry with Shanghai-style noodles.

Tofu becomes irresistible in this robust sauce of savory ground pork, spicy chile bean paste, soy sauce, and fresh green onions.

Spicy Tofu with Pork

4 tbsp soy sauce

2 tsp sesame oil

2 tsp Chinese rice wine

¼ lb (125 g) ground pork

Salt and ground white pepper

14 oz (440 g) soft tofu

½ cup (4 fl oz/125 ml) chicken stock, homemade (page 283) or purchased

1 tbsp chile bean paste

1 tsp sugar

½ tsp cornstarch

2 tbsp canola oil

3 tbsp minced green onions

1 tbsp grated fresh ginger

3 cloves garlic, minced

MAKES 4–6 SERVINGS

1 In a large nonreactive bowl, stir together 3 tbsp of the soy sauce, 1 tsp of the sesame oil, and the rice wine. Add the pork and stir to mix well. Set aside.

2 Bring a saucepan three-fourths full of water to a gentle boil over medium heat. Add 1 tbsp salt and the tofu, reduce the heat to low, and simmer for about 5 minutes to firm up the tofu. Using a slotted spoon or a wire skimmer, transfer the tofu to a plate. Weight with a second plate to press out the excess water. Set aside for 30 minutes. Just before stir-frying, pour off any water and cut the tofu into ½-inch (12-mm) cubes.

3 In a small bowl, whisk together the remaining 1 tbsp soy sauce and 1 tsp sesame oil, the stock, chile bean paste, sugar, cornstarch, and ⅛ tsp white pepper to make a braising sauce. Set aside.

4 In a large wok or frying pan over medium-high heat, warm the oil. When the oil is hot, add the pork and its marinade and stir-fry until it just turns opaque, about 2 minutes. Add 2 tbsp of the green onions, the ginger, and garlic and stir-fry until fragrant, about 1 minute. Stir in the stock mixture and simmer until the sauce begins to thicken, 2–3 minutes. Add the reserved tofu, reduce the heat to low, and simmer, uncovered, stirring occasionally and being careful to stir gently so the tofu does not fall apart, until most of the sauce is absorbed, about 10 minutes.

5 Transfer to a warmed serving bowl, garnish with the remaining 1 tbsp green onions, and serve at once.

The lightly sweet, citrus-infused sauce of this classic Chinese stir-fry pairs well with delicate jasmine rice (page 288).

Tangerine Beef Stir-Fry

1½ lb (750 g) flank steak

¾ tsp sugar

¼ tsp baking soda

Salt

¼ tsp cornstarch

1 tsp grated tangerine or orange zest

¼ cup (2 fl oz/60 ml) fresh tangerine or orange juice

1 tbsp Chinese rice wine

1 tbsp hoisin sauce

2 tbsp soy sauce

1 tsp chile bean paste

1 tsp ginger juice (page 292) or finely grated fresh ginger

½ tsp sesame oil

4 tbsp (2 fl oz/60 ml) canola oil

1 small yellow onion, halved and thinly sliced

1 small green bell pepper, seeded and thinly sliced lengthwise

1 red Fresno chile, seeded and thinly sliced lengthwise

2 cloves garlic, minced

MAKES 4–6 SERVINGS

1 Put the steak in the freezer for about 30 minutes to firm up, then cut across the grain into slices about ⅛ inch (3 mm) thick. In a large, nonreactive bowl, combine ½ tsp of the sugar, baking soda, and 1 tsp salt and stir to mix well. Add the beef slices and stir to coat. Let stand at room temperature for about 30 minutes.

2 To make the sauce, in a small bowl, whisk together the remaining ¼ sugar, the cornstarch, tangerine zest and juice, rice wine, hoisin sauce, soy sauce, chile bean paste, ginger juice, and sesame oil. Set aside.

3 Pat the beef slices dry with paper towels. In a large wok or frying pan over high heat, warm 2 tbsp of the canola oil. Add half of the beef in a single layer and sear until brown on the first side, about 1 minute. Using tongs, turn to sear until brown on the other side, about 30 seconds. Transfer the meat to a colander to drain. Return the pan to high heat, warm 1 tbsp of the canola oil, and repeat to sear the remaining beef. Transfer the second batch of beef to the colander to drain.

4 Wipe the wok clean. Reheat over high heat and add the remaining 1 tbsp oil. When the oil is hot, add the onion and bell pepper and stir-fry until the edges begin to brown, 3–4 minutes. Add the chile and garlic and stir-fry for about 1 minute. Give the sauce a quick stir, add to the pan along with the beef, and stir-fry until the beef is heated through and the sauce thickens, about 1 minute. Transfer to a warmed bowl or platter and serve at once.

A mainstay of numerous Chinese restaurant menus, this comforting noodle dish is a delicious way to eat your vegetables.

Vegetable Chow Mein

½ lb (250 g) fresh Chinese egg noodles

5 tbsp (3 fl oz/80 ml) canola or peanut oil

2 tbsp *each* oyster sauce, soy sauce, and rice vinegar

1 tbsp sesame oil

1 tsp sugar

½ yellow onion, thinly sliced

1 red bell pepper, seeded and thinly sliced lengthwise

¼ lb (125 g) shiitake mushrooms, stemmed and thinly sliced

1 zucchini, trimmed and cut into matchsticks

1 tbsp grated fresh ginger

2 cloves garlic, minced

MAKES 4 SERVINGS

1 Bring a large pot three-fourths full of water to a boil. Add the noodles, cook for 2 minutes, drain, and rinse well with running cold water. Place in a bowl, add 1 tbsp of the canola oil, and toss to coat evenly. Set aside.

2 To make the sauce, in another bowl, whisk together 3 tbsp water and the oyster sauce, soy sauce, vinegar, sesame oil, and sugar. Set aside.

3 Heat a wok or large frying pan over high heat until very hot and add 2 tbsp of the canola oil. Add the onion and bell pepper and stir-fry just until tender, about 2 minutes. Add the mushrooms and zucchini and continue to stir-fry until golden brown, about 2 minutes. Using a slotted spoon, transfer the vegetables to a bowl.

4 Return the wok to high heat and add the remaining 2 tbsp oil. Add the ginger and garlic and stir-fry until fragrant, about 5 seconds. Add the noodles and cook until heated through, about 5 minutes. Return the vegetables to the pan, add the sauce, and continue to stir-fry until all the ingredients are well combined and heated through, about 1 minute. Transfer to a warm serving platter. Serve at once.

NOTE For a heartier dish, add peeled and deveined shrimp or strips of boneless, skinless chicken breast or pork loin to the pan after stir-frying the ginger and garlic. Toss until cooked through before proceeding.

Introduced in Hong Kong, these bright yellow custard-filled tartlets probably evolved from Portuguese or English tarts.

Egg Custard Tartlets

Tartlet Dough (page 289)

⅓ cup (3 fl oz/80 ml) whole milk

2 eggs plus 1 egg yolk

⅓ cup (3 oz/90 g) sugar

Pinch of salt

1 tsp fresh lemon juice

½ tsp pure vanilla extract

MAKES 12 TARTLETS

1 Prepare the dough as directed. Turn the dough out onto a lightly floured work surface and form into a cylinder 12 inches (30 cm) long. Cut the cylinder crosswise into 12 equal pieces. Have ready 12 tartlet pans, each 3 inches (7.5 cm) in diameter and 1–1½ inches (2.5–4 cm) deep. Press each piece of dough evenly into the bottom and up the sides of a pan. Place the dough-lined pans on a baking sheet and refrigerate until the dough sets, at least 1 hour or up to overnight.

2 Preheat the oven to 325°F (165°C). Lightly prick the bottom of each dough-lined pan with a fork and bake on the baking sheet until light golden brown, 15 minutes. Let cool on the baking sheet while you prepare the filling.

3 To make the filling, in a saucepan over medium heat, combine the milk and 2 tbsp water. Bring to a boil, then remove from the heat. In a bowl, whisk together the whole eggs and egg yolk, sugar, salt, and lemon juice until well combined, 1–2 minutes. Whisking continuously, gradually pour the hot milk mixture into the eggs in a slow, steady stream. Stir in the vanilla. Pour the custard through a fine-mesh sieve into a measuring pitcher or another bowl.

4 Pour the custard into the baked tartlet shells, filling each to within ⅛ inch (3 mm) of the rim. Bake until the centers are just set, 15–20 minutes. The custard filling should not brown; it will puff up then flatten when the tartlets cool. Remove the tartlets from the oven and let stand on the baking sheet until they are cool to the touch, then remove from the pans and serve.

Thai & Vietnamese

Rice-paper rounds—dried translucent sheets made from rice flour—become tender wrappers for delicious fillings when soaked.

Fresh Spring Rolls with Shrimp

Salt

6 medium shrimp, peeled and deveined (page 292)

2 oz (60 g) cellophane noodles, soaked in boiling water for 15 minutes

6 rice-paper rounds, each about 8 inches (20 cm) in diameter

6 red-leaf or butter lettuce leaves, stems removed

1 small carrot, shredded

½ small cucumber, peeled, seeded, and shredded

½ cup (½ oz/15 g) mung bean sprouts

18 *each* fresh mint leaves and fresh cilantro leaves

Chile-Lime Dipping Sauce (page 285) for serving

MAKES 6 SPRING ROLLS

1 Bring a saucepan three-fourths full of salted water to a boil. Add the shrimp and return to a boil. Reduce the heat to medium and simmer just until the shrimp turn bright pink and opaque, about 2 minutes. Drain and let cool. Cut each shrimp in half lengthwise.

2 To assemble the rolls, drain the noodles. Fill a wide, shallow bowl with warm water. Working with 1 rice-paper round at a time, soak it in the warm water until softened, 5 or 6 seconds. Remove it from the bowl, gently shake off the excess water, and place it on a work surface. Place a lettuce leaf horizontally on the bottom half of the moistened rice paper. In a line across the base of the lettuce, place 1 tsp of the carrot, 1 tsp of the cucumber, several noodle strands, and several bean sprouts. Be careful not to overstuff the rolls. Lift the bottom edge of the rice paper and carefully roll up halfway into a tight cylinder. Place 2 shrimp halves and several mint and cilantro leaves in a line along the inside seam of the roll. Fold in the sides of the rice paper and continue to roll the rice paper and filling into a cylinder. Moisten the edge of the roll to seal.

3 Repeat with the remaining ingredients. Place the prepared rolls, seam side down, on a platter and cover with plastic wrap until ready to serve. The rolls will keep at room temperature for several hours before serving. To serve, cut the rolls in half on the diagonal and accompany with the dipping sauce.

Satay, highly seasoned meat woven onto skewers and grilled, is typically served with a smooth and savory peanut sauce.

Chicken Satay

⅓ cup (3 fl oz/80 ml) plus ½ cup (4 fl oz/125 ml) coconut milk

¼ cup (2 fl oz/60 ml) fish sauce

2 tbsp firmly packed golden brown sugar

1 tbsp Madras curry powder

6 cloves garlic, minced

1 tbsp minced fresh ginger

1 tbsp minced fresh cilantro

2 lb (1 kg) skinless, boneless chicken thighs, cut into strips about 3 inches (7.5 cm) long by 1 inch (2.5 cm) wide

2 tbsp canola oil, plus extra for brushing

2 tbsp minced shallots

¼ cup (2½ oz/75 g) creamy peanut butter

2 tbsp tamarind paste (optional)

1 tbsp chile paste

Salt

¼ cup (1¼ oz/35 g) minced unsalted dry-roasted peanuts

MAKES 4–6 SERVINGS

1 In a large nonreactive bowl, combine the ⅓ cup coconut milk, the fish sauce, brown sugar, curry powder, half of the minced garlic, the ginger, and cilantro and stir to mix well. Add the chicken strips and stir to coat thoroughly. Cover and marinate in the refrigerator for at least 1 hour or up to overnight.

2 Soak 24–32 bamboo skewers, each 8 inches (20 cm) long, in cold water to cover for at least 30 minutes.

3 To make the peanut sauce, in a saucepan over medium heat, warm the 2 tbsp oil. Add the shallots and the remaining half of the minced garlic and sauté until fragrant, about 1 minute. Reduce the heat to low and add the ½ cup coconut milk, peanut butter, tamarind paste (if using), chile paste, ¼ tsp salt, and ¼ cup (2 fl oz/60 ml) water. Cook, stirring constantly, until the sauce begins to simmer and thicken, about 2 minutes. Add the peanuts and mix well. Transfer the peanut sauce to a bowl and set aside.

4 Prepare a gas or charcoal grill for direct grilling over high heat (page 293). Oil the grill rack. Remove the chicken strips from the marinade. Discard the marinade. Thread the chicken strips lengthwise onto the skewers.

5 Place the skewers directly over the heat elements or over the hottest part of the fire. Sear the chicken, turning once, until golden brown on both sides, 2–3 minutes per side. Move the skewers to an area of the grill with less heat, cover the grill, and cook until the chicken is opaque throughout, about 5 minutes longer. Arrange the skewers on a platter and serve at once with the peanut sauce.

This popular Thai-style salad is bursting with the vibrant flavors typical of Thai cuisine: lime, fresh herbs, and spicy chiles.

Thai Beef Salad

3 tbsp *each* fish sauce and lime juice

2 tsp sugar

1–2 tsp minced fresh hot chiles

2 tsp canola oil, plus extra as needed

1 lb (500 g) flank steak

Salt and freshly ground pepper

1 large head butter lettuce, torn into bite-sized pieces

1 cup (5 oz/155 g) thinly sliced English cucumber

½ cup (2 oz/60 g) thinly sliced sweet or red onion

½ cup (2½ oz/75 g) thin strips red bell pepper

½ cup (¾ oz/20 g) *each* lightly packed torn fresh mint leaves and cilantro leaves

¼ cup (⅓ oz/10 g) lightly packed torn fresh Thai or sweet basil leaves (optional)

MAKES 4 SERVINGS

1 To make the vinaigrette, in a large bowl, stir together the fish sauce, lime juice, sugar, and chiles to taste. Set aside.

2 Prepare a gas or charcoal grill for direct grilling over high heat (page 293), or preheat a broiler. Oil the grill rack or broiler pan. Sprinkle the flank steak evenly with salt and pepper and rub the seasoning into the meat. Brush the steak lightly on both sides with the 2 tsp oil.

3 If using a grill, place the flank steak directly over the heat elements or the hottest part of the fire. If using the broiler, place the flank steak on a broiler pan and slide it under the broiler about 2 inches (5 cm) from the heat source.

4 Grill or broil the steak, turning once with tongs, until seared on the outside and cooked rare to medium-rare in the center, about 4 minutes per side. Transfer the steak to a cutting board and let rest for about 10 minutes. Cut the steak across the grain on the diagonal into very thin slices.

5 Add the butter lettuce, cucumber, onion, bell pepper, mint, cilantro, and Thai basil, if using, to the bowl with the vinaigrette and toss to coat evenly. Divide the salad among individual plates, arrange the meat on top of each salad, and serve at once.

Pickled Cucumber Salad

2 lb (1 kg) cucumbers

Salt

½ cup (4 fl oz/125 ml)
rice vinegar

2 tbsp sugar

4 shallots, thinly sliced

1 red Fresno chile, seeded
and cut into thin rings

2 tbsp chopped fresh cilantro

MAKES 4–6 SERVINGS

1 Peel the cucumbers and cut each in half lengthwise. Using the tip of a spoon, scrape out the seeds. Cut each half crosswise into slices about ¼ inch (6 mm) thick. Place the cucumber slices in a colander, sprinkle with 1 tsp salt, and toss to mix well. Set aside at room temperature and let drain for 1 hour.

2 In a small saucepan, combine the vinegar, sugar, and 1 tsp salt. Bring to a simmer over medium heat and cook, stirring to dissolve the sugar, for 2 minutes. Set aside and let cool to room temperature.

3 Pat the cucumbers dry with paper towels. In a large bowl, combine the cucumbers, shallots, chile, and cilantro and toss to mix well. Pour the vinegar mixture over the cucumber mixture and toss to coat thoroughly. Cover and refrigerate for at least 2 hours or up to overnight. Serve chilled.

This simple salad is the perfect accompaniment to grilled meats such as Chicken Satay (page 251).

Thai Chicken Soup

1 small orange

3 cups (24 fl oz/750 ml) coconut milk

1½ cups (12 fl oz/375 ml) chicken stock, homemade (page 283) or purchased

2 tsp fish sauce

2 skinless, boneless chicken breast halves, cut into cubes

6 oz (185 g) button mushrooms, quartered

Juice from 1 lime

Salt and freshly ground pepper

¼ cup (⅓ oz/10 g) minced fresh Thai or regular basil

MAKES 4 SERVINGS

1 Grate 1 tbsp zest and extract ½ cup (4 fl oz/125 ml) juice from the orange. In a saucepan over medium-high heat, combine the orange juice and zest, coconut milk, stock, and fish sauce. Stir well and bring to a boil. Reduce the heat to low, add the chicken, and simmer, uncovered, for 5 minutes.

2 Add the mushrooms to the soup and continue to cook until the chicken is opaque throughout and the mushrooms are tender, about 5 minutes longer. Add the lime juice and season to taste with salt and pepper. Ladle into bowls, garnish with the basil, and serve at once.

This comforting chicken and coconut soup brings together the flavors of the Thai kitchen in perfect balance.

This crunchy, colorful salad is a mainstay on both Thai and Vietnamese tables. Jicama can be substituted for the green papaya.

Green Papaya Salad

1 large green papaya, about 1½ lb (750 g), peeled, halved, and seeded

1 carrot, peeled

4 shallots, thinly sliced, plus 1 tbsp chopped

1 red Fresno chile, seeded and cut into thin rings

2 tbsp chopped fresh cilantro

2 cloves garlic, chopped

1 tsp sugar

¼ cup (2 fl oz/60 ml) *each* rice vinegar and fish sauce

2 tbsp *each* fresh lime juice and chile-garlic sauce such as Sriracha

3 tbsp canola oil

MAKES 4–6 SERVINGS

1 Using the largest holes on a grater-shredder or a mandoline, and holding each papaya half lengthwise, shred the flesh into long, thin strips. Shred the carrot into long, thin strips.

2 In a large bowl, combine the shredded papaya, shredded carrot, sliced shallots, chile, and cilantro and toss gently to mix well.

3 To make the dressing, in a mini food processor or mortar, combine the chopped shallot, garlic, and sugar and process or grind with a pestle until a smooth paste forms. Add 1–2 tsp water if needed. Transfer the garlic paste to a bowl and whisk in the vinegar, fish sauce, lime juice, and chile-garlic sauce. Gradually drizzle in the oil while continuing to whisk.

4 Pour the dressing over the papaya mixture and toss to coat thoroughly. Refrigerate for at least 2 hours or up to overnight before serving.

Here, stir-fried rice noodles in a sweet and tangy sauce are topped with tender shrimp, crunchy bean sprouts, and salty peanuts.

Pad Thai

2 red Fresno chiles, seeded and chopped

2 shallots, chopped

3 cloves garlic, chopped

½ lb (250 g) dried flat rice noodles

3 tbsp tamarind paste (optional)

2 eggs

Salt and freshly ground pepper

2 tbsp plus 1 tsp canola oil

¼ cup (2 fl oz/60 ml) fish sauce

2 tbsp soy sauce

2 tbsp firmly packed golden brown sugar

2 tbsp fresh lime juice

½ lb (250 g) shrimp, peeled and deveined (page 292), then chopped

1¼ cups (1½ oz/45 g) mung bean sprouts

½ cup (4 fl oz/125 ml) chicken stock, homemade (page 283) or purchased

2 tbsp chopped unsalted dry-roasted peanuts

Fresh cilantro sprigs for garnish

MAKES 4–6 SERVINGS

1 In a mini food processor, process the chiles, shallots, garlic, and 1 tbsp water until a thick paste forms. Place the noodles in a bowl and add warm water to cover. Let stand for 15 minutes. Drain the noodles and set aside. If using tamarind paste and it is dense, soak it in a little hot water and then pass it through a fine-mesh sieve, discarding the seeds and fibers.

2 In a bowl, beat the eggs with ⅛ tsp salt and a pinch of pepper until thoroughly combined. In an 8-inch (20-cm) nonstick frying pan over medium heat, warm the 1 tsp oil. Pour in the egg mixture and cook just until the edges begin to set, 2–3 seconds. Using the spatula, pull the cooked egg toward the center, then tilt the pan so that the uncooked egg runs to the edges. Repeat until the omelet is just set but still moist on the surface, about 20 seconds. Slide the omelet onto a cutting board and let cool for about 5 minutes. Cut the omelet in half and stack the halves, then slice into thin strips.

3 In a large wok or frying pan over medium-high heat, warm the 2 tbsp oil. Add the reserved chile paste and sauté until fragrant, about 10 seconds. Stir in the fish sauce, tamarind paste (if using), soy sauce, brown sugar, and lime juice. Add the shrimp and stir-fry just until they turn pink, about 1 minute.

4 Add the reserved noodles to the wok along with 1 cup (1 oz/30 g) of the bean sprouts and the stock. Bring the stock to a boil, reduce the heat to low, cover, and cook, stirring 2 or 3 times, until most of the sauce has been absorbed by the noodles, about 6 minutes.

5 Transfer the noodle mixture to a warmed platter. Top with the omelet strips, remaining bean sprouts, peanuts, and cilantro. Serve at once.

An ideal side dish to this citrusy Thai curry is a refreshing Green Papaya Salad (page 257). Try it with fish or shrimp only, instead of a mixture.

Seafood-Coconut Curry

3 dried red Thai chiles

2 shallots, chopped

2 tbsp chopped fresh ginger

3 cloves garlic, chopped

1 stalk lemongrass, tender midsection only, chopped

1 tbsp chopped fresh cilantro, plus extra for garnish

2 red Fresno chiles, seeded and chopped

4 kaffir lime leaves, spines removed (optional)

½ tsp shrimp paste (optional)

1 tbsp unsweetened flaked coconut

1½ cups (12 fl oz/375 ml) coconut cream (page 294) or coconut milk

4½ tsp fish sauce

1 tbsp *each* brown sugar and lime juice

½ lb (250 g) sea bass fillets

½ lb (250 g) scallops

½ lb (250 g) medium shrimp, peeled and deveined (page 292), tail segments intact

MAKES 4–6 SERVINGS

1 Soak the dried chiles in warm water for 15 minutes, then drain. To make the curry paste, in a mini food processor or mortar, combine the shallots, ginger, garlic, lemongrass, cilantro, fresh and soaked dried chiles, the lime leaves (if using), shrimp paste (if using), and flaked coconut and process or grind with a pestle until a smooth paste forms. Add 1–2 tbsp water if needed to facilitate the grinding.

2 In a Dutch oven or large, heavy pot, bring the coconut cream to a simmer over medium heat. Cook for 2 minutes. Add the curry paste and return to a simmer, stirring to dissolve the curry paste. Cook until the mixture thickens slightly, about 3 minutes. Add the fish sauce, brown sugar, and lime juice and cook, stirring occasionally, until the flavors are blended, 7–10 minutes longer. Taste and adjust the seasoning.

3 Cut the sea bass into pieces about 2 inches (5 cm) long and ½ inch (12 mm) wide. Cut the scallops into quarters. Stir the fish, scallops, and shrimp into the coconut curry. Simmer very gently over medium-low heat until the seafood is opaque throughout, 5–7 minutes. Be careful not to allow the liquid to come to a full boil. Transfer to a warmed bowl, garnish with cilantro, and serve at once.

Here, gently simmered catfish is flavored with turmeric, lime, and garlic, and then served over noodles for a colorful result.

Braised Fish with Lime & Garlic

5 tbsp (3 fl oz/80 ml) canola oil

2 tbsp fresh lime juice

1 tbsp ground turmeric

Salt and freshly ground pepper

1 lb (500 g) catfish fillets, cut into pieces 2 inches (5 cm) long and ½ inch (12 mm) wide

6 oz (185 g) dried rice vermicelli, soaked in hot water for 15 minutes then drained

4 shallots, thinly sliced

3 cloves garlic, minced

1 tbsp *each* chopped fresh dill and chopped fresh cilantro

1 green onion, thinly sliced on the diagonal

1 tbsp chopped unsalted dry-roasted peanuts

Chile-Lime Dipping Sauce (page 285) for serving

MAKES 4–6 SERVINGS

1 In a large nonreactive bowl, whisk together 3 tbsp of the oil, the lime juice, turmeric, 1 tsp salt, and ¼ tsp pepper. Add the catfish pieces and stir to coat thoroughly. Let marinate at room temperature for 30 minutes or cover and refrigerate for up to 1 hour.

2 Bring a large saucepan three-fourths full of water to a boil. Separate the strands of noodles. Add them to the boiling water, cook for 30 seconds, then drain and transfer to a warmed serving bowl. Keep the noodles warm.

3 In a large nonstick frying pan over medium-high heat, warm the remaining 2 tbsp oil. Add the shallots and sauté until translucent, about 1 minute. Add the garlic and pour the catfish with its marinade into the pan. Reduce the heat to medium-low, spread the fish in a single layer, and simmer until the fish is opaque on the first side, 3–4 minutes. Using a spatula, carefully turn the fish. Stir in the dill and cilantro and simmer until the fish is opaque throughout, about 3 minutes longer.

4 To serve, pour the catfish and sauce over the noodles. Garnish with the green onion and peanuts and serve at once with the dipping sauce.

This comforting and hearty Vietnamese-style curry features fork-tender chicken bathed in a creamy coconut sauce.

Chicken in Yellow Curry

3 tbsp canola oil

3 lb (1.5 kg) skinless, bone-in chicken thighs

3 cloves garlic, minced

2 shallots, minced

3 tbsp Madras curry powder

1 tbsp firmly packed dark brown sugar

1 tsp red pepper flakes

Freshly ground black pepper

2 stalks lemongrass, tender midsections only, trimmed and cut into 1-inch (2.5-cm) pieces

1-inch (2.5-cm) piece fresh ginger, cut into 4 slices

1 cup (8 fl oz/250 ml) chicken stock, homemade (page 283) or purchased

1 can (13½ fl oz/420 ml) coconut milk

2 tbsp fish sauce

3 carrots, cut into chunks

1 sweet potato, about ¾ lb (375 g), peeled and cut into chunks

3 tbsp thinly sliced fresh Thai or regular basil leaves

MAKES 6–8 SERVINGS

1 In a Dutch oven or large, heavy pot over medium-high heat, warm the oil. Working in batches if necessary, sear the chicken thighs until nicely browned, about 4 minutes per side. Remove from the pan with tongs and set aside.

2 Add the garlic and shallots to the pot and sauté over medium-high heat just until fragrant, about 30 seconds. Add the curry powder, brown sugar, red pepper flakes, 1 tsp black pepper, the lemongrass, and ginger and sauté until the spices are fragrant and well blended with the garlic and shallots, about 30 seconds. Add the stock and deglaze the pot, scraping the bottom with a wooden spoon to dislodge any browned bits. Stir in the coconut milk and fish sauce and bring to a boil.

3 Add the chicken thighs, carrots, and sweet potato to the pot, pushing them into the coconut milk mixture. Partially cover the pot and cook over low heat until the chicken is opaque throughout and the chicken and vegetables are very tender, about 1 hour.

4 Transfer the chicken, vegetables, and sauce to a warmed platter. Garnish with the basil and serve at once.

The iconic Southeast-Asian flavors of this grilled chicken dish are delicious with steamed Coconut Rice (page 288).

Grilled Garlic Chicken

2 shallots, chopped

4 cloves garlic, chopped

1 tbsp chopped fresh ginger

2 tbsp chopped fresh cilantro stems

Freshly ground pepper

⅓ cup (3 fl oz/80 ml) coconut milk

2 tbsp fish sauce

1 tbsp soy sauce

1 tbsp rice wine

1 tbsp firmly packed dark brown sugar

1 tbsp canola oil, plus extra for brushing

1 chicken, about 3½ lb (1.75 kg), halved (page 293)

Chile-Lime Dipping Sauce (page 285) for serving

MAKES 4–6 SERVINGS

1 In a mini food processor or mortar, combine the shallots, garlic, ginger, cilantro, and ¼ tsp pepper and process or grind with a pestle until a smooth paste forms. Add 1–2 tbsp water if needed to facilitate the grinding. Transfer to a bowl. Add the coconut milk, fish sauce, soy sauce, rice wine, brown sugar, and oil and stir to mix well. Pour the marinade into a large zippered plastic bag, add the chicken halves, seal the bag, and massage to coat the chicken with the mixture. Refrigerate for at least 4 hours or up to overnight.

2 Prepare a gas or charcoal grill for direct grilling over high heat (page 293). Oil the grill rack. Remove the chicken from the marinade and shake off the excess. Discard the marinade. Place the chicken halves, skin side up, directly over the heat elements or over the hottest part of the fire. Sear until golden brown on both sides, turning once, 7–9 minutes. Using tongs, move the chicken to an area of the grill with less heat. Cover and continue to cook until the juices run clear when a thigh is pierced, 20–25 minutes.

3 Remove the chicken from the grill, cover loosely with aluminum foil, and let rest for 10 minutes. Cut each chicken half into 5 or 6 pieces, halving the thigh and breast. Transfer to a warmed platter. Serve at once accompanied by the chile-lime dipping sauce.

Spicy Minced Chicken

1 lb (500 g) skinless, boneless chicken thighs, cut into 2-inch (5-cm) cubes

2 tbsp canola oil

3 shallots, thinly sliced

1 red or green serrano chile, seeded and cut into thin rings

2 tbsp chopped fresh cilantro

2 tbsp chopped fresh mint

Spicy Thai Dressing (page 286)

6–8 red-leaf lettuce leaves, stems removed

¼ cup (1½ oz/45 g) chopped unsalted dry-roasted peanuts

MAKES 4–6 SERVINGS

1 Put the cubed chicken in the freezer for 15 minutes to firm it up. Remove the chicken from the freezer and place in a food processor. Process just until uniformly and finely minced, about 10 seconds. Do not overprocess or the meat will become mushy.

2 In a large nonstick frying pan over medium-high heat, warm the oil. Add the minced chicken and sauté, using a wooden spoon to break up the meat, until opaque throughout, 4–5 minutes. Scrape into a fine-mesh sieve and drain thoroughly, then transfer to a large bowl. Add the sliced shallots, chile, cilantro, and mint and toss gently to mix.

3 Pour the dressing over the chicken mixture and toss to coat thoroughly. Line individual plates or a platter with the lettuce. Divide the chicken mixture among the leaves and garnish with the peanuts. Serve at room temperature.

This deservedly popular Thai salad, called *larb gai,* features minced meat flavored with herbs, fish sauce, chile-garlic sauce, and lime.

Stir-Fried Pork with Garlic

1½ lb (750 g) pork shoulder

1½ tsp sugar

Salt and freshly ground pepper

¼ tsp baking soda

3 tbsp chicken broth

2 tbsp soy sauce

1 tsp rice vinegar

½ tsp cornstarch

2 tbsp canola oil

4 cloves garlic, minced

1 handful fresh Thai or regular basil leaves

Coconut Rice or Steamed Rice (page 288) for serving

MAKES 4–6 SERVINGS

1 Put the pork in the freezer for about 30 minutes to firm up, then thinly slice against the grain into pieces 2 inches (5 cm) long. In a large nonreactive bowl, combine ½ tsp of the sugar, ¼ tsp salt, and the baking soda and stir to mix well. Add the pork slices and stir to coat well. Let marinate at room temperature for about 30 minutes.

2 To make the sauce, in a bowl, whisk together the broth, soy sauce, vinegar, cornstarch, the remaining 1 tsp sugar, and ¼ tsp pepper. Set aside.

3 In a large wok or frying pan over high heat, warm the oil. When the oil is hot, add the garlic and sauté until just beginning to turn golden brown, about 10 seconds. Working quickly, add the pork to the pan and stir-fry until the meat is crisp and just turns opaque, about 1 minute. Stir in the sauce and sauté until it thickens, about 10 seconds. Stir in the basil leaves just until they wilt. Transfer to a warmed platter and serve at once with the rice.

Only a handful of ingredients add vibrant flavor to this stir-fry, which is simple enough for a weeknight.

The key to fragrant Thai red curries is the paste made from red chiles. When you're in a hurry, use purchased red curry paste.

Red Curry Beef

1 lb (500 g) beef tenderloin

¼ cup (2 fl oz/60 ml) fish sauce

1½ tbsp firmly packed
dark brown sugar

1 tsp tamarind paste (optional)

1 tsp fresh lime juice

2 tbsp canola oil

1 small yellow onion,
halved and thinly sliced

1 small red bell pepper,
seeded and thinly sliced

1 cup (8 fl oz/250 ml)
coconut milk

½ cup (4 oz/125 g) Thai Red
Curry Paste (page 286)
or 2 tbsp purchased
red curry paste

1 tbsp chopped unsalted
dry-roasted peanuts

8–10 fresh Thai or
regular basil leaves

Steamed Rice (page 288)
for serving

MAKES 4–6 SERVINGS

1 Put the beef in the freezer for 30 minutes to firm up, then cut against the grain into slices about ⅛ inch (3 mm) thick. Set aside.

2 In a small bowl, stir together the fish sauce, brown sugar, tamarind paste (if using), and lime juice. Set aside.

3 In a Dutch oven or large, heavy pot over high heat, warm the oil. Add the onion and red bell pepper and stir-fry until just tender, about 5 minutes. Add the coconut milk and heat just until it begins to bubble. Stir in the curry paste, bring to a simmer, and cook for about 5 minutes. Add the reserved fish sauce mixture and simmer until the curry thickens, 7–10 minutes.

4 Reduce the heat to low, add the beef slices, and simmer until the beef is almost cooked through but still pink in the center, 5–7 minutes longer. Transfer the curry to a warmed bowl, garnish with the peanuts and basil, and serve at once accompanied by the rice.

This refreshing Vietnamese salad can be topped with other grilled meats or seafood, such as chicken, pork, or prawns.

Lemongrass Beef & Rice Vermicelli

¾ lb (375 g) rice vermicelli

1 lb (500 g) beef chuck or flank steak

3 stalks lemongrass, tender midsection only, minced

5 cloves garlic, minced

1½ tbsp fish sauce

½ tsp sugar

Freshly ground pepper

½ English cucumber, peeled, seeded, and shredded

4 cups (4 oz/125 g) finely shredded romaine lettuce

2 cups (4 oz/125 g) bean sprouts

1 carrot, peeled and shredded

½ cup (¾ oz/20 g) *each* finely shredded Thai or regular basil and fresh mint leaves

3 tbsp canola oil, or as needed

1 large red onion, thinly sliced

½ cup (3 oz/90 g) chopped unsalted roasted peanuts

Chile-Lime Dipping Sauce (page 285) for serving

MAKES 4 SERVINGS

1 Soak the noodles in warm water to cover for 15 minutes. Meanwhile, bring a pot three-fourths full of water to a boil. Drain the noodles, add to the boiling water, stir well, and boil until tender, 2–3 minutes. Pour into a colander, rinse thoroughly with running cold water, and drain again. Set aside.

2 Put the beef in the freezer for 30 minutes to firm up, then cut against the grain into thin slices. In a bowl, combine the beef, lemongrass, half of the garlic, the fish sauce, sugar, and pepper to taste. Mix well, cover, and set aside.

3 Toss together the cucumber, lettuce, bean sprouts, carrot, basil, and mint. Divide the mixture evenly among 4 shallow bowls. Top each salad with an equal amount of the noodles. Set aside.

4 In a wok or large frying pan over medium-high heat, warm the 3 tbsp oil. Add the remaining garlic and stir-fry until golden, about 30 seconds. Add the onion and stir-fry until the layers separate, about 30 seconds longer. Push the onion and garlic up the sides of the pan. Add additional oil if the pan is dry. Add a batch of the beef mixture and spread it over the bottom of the pan. Cook without stirring until the beef is nicely seared on the bottom, about 1 minute. Turn over and sear the other side, 1 minute longer. Transfer to a plate. Fry the remaining beef mixture in batches.

5 When all of the beef is seared, return it to the wok and stir and toss for a few seconds to reheat. Divide the beef mixture evenly among the salads. Garnish with the peanuts. Pour the dipping sauce into individual bowls to serve alongside each salad. Diners can add as much sauce as they like.

This zesty Vietnamese salad gets its name from juicy steak being seared and "shaken" in a hot pan until crisp and browned.

"Shaking" Beef

2 tbsp canola oil

2 tbsp fish sauce

6 cloves garlic, minced

1½ tsp sugar

Freshly ground pepper

1 lb (500 g) beef tenderloin, cut into 1-inch (2.5-cm) cubes

2 tbsp fresh lime juice

1 tbsp rice vinegar

1 tbsp soy sauce

½ small yellow onion, sliced paper-thin

2 green onions, white and pale green parts, thinly sliced

2 cups (2 oz/60 g) loosely packed watercress or arugula, tough stems removed

MAKES 4–6 SERVINGS

1 To make the marinade, in a large, nonreactive bowl, combine 1 tbsp of the oil, 1 tbsp of the fish sauce, half of the garlic, ½ tsp of the sugar, and ⅛ tsp pepper and stir to mix well. Add the beef and stir to coat thoroughly. Cover and refrigerate for at least 2 hours or up to overnight.

2 To make the sauce, in a small bowl, whisk together the lime juice, vinegar, soy sauce, the remaining 1 tbsp fish sauce and 1 tsp sugar, and ⅛ tsp pepper. Put the onion slices in another bowl and drizzle with 1 tbsp of the sauce. Set the onions and the remaining sauce aside.

3 In a large wok or frying pan over high heat, warm the remaining 1 tbsp oil. Add the beef and stir-fry until browned, 4–5 minutes. Add the green onions and the remaining garlic and stir-fry just until fragrant, a few seconds. Remove the pan from the heat, pour in the remaining sauce, and toss to mix.

4 To serve, toss the watercress with the marinated sliced onions and mound on a platter. Using a slotted spoon, spoon the beef over the greens and then drizzle the pan juices over the beef. Serve at once.

Thai red tea leaves premixed with aromatic star anise, cinnamon sticks, and vanilla can be found at many Asian markets.

Thai Iced Tea

½ cup (½ oz/15 g) Thai red tea mix or loose-leaf jasmine tea

½ cup (4 fl oz/125 ml) half-and-half

⅓ cup (3 fl oz/80 ml) sweetened condensed milk

2 tbsp sugar

Ice cubes for serving

MAKES 4 SERVINGS

1 In a saucepan over medium heat, bring 4 cups (32 fl oz/1 l) water to a boil. Add the tea, turn off the heat, and let steep for 5–7 minutes. Strain the tea through a very fine-mesh sieve or a sieve lined with cheesecloth into a heatproof pitcher. Let cool to room temperature.

2 Meanwhile, in a measuring pitcher, whisk together the half-and-half, condensed milk, and sugar.

3 To serve, divide the ice among 4 tall glasses. Pour the sweetened milk over the ice, dividing it evenly. Slowly fill the glasses with the brewed tea, keeping the tea separate from the milk. Provide long spoons for stirring the milk and tea together before drinking.

A staple in Thailand, sticky, or glutinous, rice is used in desserts like this delicious medley of mango with coconut sauce.

Sticky Rice with Mango

2 cups (14 oz/440 g) glutinous rice, rinsed

⅔ cup (5 fl oz/160 ml) coconut milk, plus 1 cup (8 fl oz/250 ml) coconut cream (page 294) or coconut milk

⅓ cup (3 oz/90 g) granulated sugar

Salt

½ cup (4 oz/125 g) firmly packed golden brown sugar

2 ripe mangoes, peeled and sliced (page 290)

1 tbsp unsweetened flaked coconut, toasted (page 290)

MAKES 4–6 SERVINGS

1 In a large saucepan over high heat, bring 6 cups (48 fl oz/1.5 l) water to a boil. Pour the rice into the boiling water, turn off the heat, and let stand for about 30 minutes.

2 Pour water to a depth of 3 inches (7.5 cm) into a large saucepan. Line a steamer insert with a double layer of cheesecloth; the cheesecloth should be larger than the diameter of the steamer. Place the insert in the saucepan. The water should not touch the bottom of the steamer. Drain the rice, place it in the lined steamer, and drape the excess cheesecloth loosely over the rice. Cover the pot and steam the rice for 20 minutes. Carefully remove the cheesecloth packet, line the steamer with a fresh double layer of cheesecloth, and invert the rice back into the steamer. Drape the excess cheesecloth over the rice and steam for 15 minutes longer.

3 In a saucepan, combine the ⅔ cup coconut milk, granulated sugar, and ⅛ tsp salt. Bring to a simmer over low heat and stir until the sugar dissolves, 2–3 minutes. Transfer the cooked rice to a large bowl and gradually pour in the coconut milk mixture while gently mixing with a spatula. Cover with plastic wrap and let stand at room temperature for at least 30 minutes or up to 3 hours. Do not refrigerate the rice.

4 To make the coconut sauce, in a small saucepan, combine the 1 cup coconut cream or milk and the brown sugar. Bring to a simmer over low heat and stir until the sugar dissolves, 2–3 minutes. Set aside to cool.

5 Scoop out the rice and divide among individual plates. Using a fork, poke several holes into the top of each mound of rice. Drizzle with the coconut sauce. Garnish with the sliced mangoes and toasted coconut. Serve at once.

Basic Recipes

Beef Stock

6 lb (3 kg) meaty beef and veal shanks

2 yellow onions, coarsely chopped

1 leek, including about 6 inches (15 cm)
of the green tops, coarsely chopped

2 carrots, coarsely chopped

1 rib celery, coarsely chopped

6 cloves garlic

4 sprigs fresh flat-leaf parsley

3 sprigs fresh thyme

2 small bay leaves

10 black peppercorns

MAKES 4–5 QT (4–5 L)

In a stockpot or large, heavy pot, combine the beef and veal shanks and add cold water to cover. Place the pot over medium-high heat and slowly bring almost to a boil. Using a large spoon, skim off any scum and froth from the surface. Reduce the heat to low and simmer, uncovered, skimming the surface as needed and adding more water if necessary to keep the shanks immersed, for 2 hours.

Add the onions, leek, carrots, celery, garlic, parsley, thyme, bay leaves, and peppercorns and continue to simmer over low heat, uncovered, until the meat begins to fall from the bones and the stock is very flavorful, about 2 hours longer.

Remove from the heat and let stand until the liquid is almost at room temperature, about 1 hour. Using a slotted spoon, lift out the meat and reserve for another use, if desired. Pour the stock through a fine-mesh sieve into a large vessel, then discard the solids. Line the sieve with cheesecloth and strain again, pouring it into 1 or 2 containers with tight-fitting lids.

Let the stock cool to room temperature, then cover and refrigerate until chilled. Using a spoon, lift off the congealed layer of fat on top and discard. Refrigerate the stock for up to 5 days or freeze for up to 2 months.

Chicken Stock

5 lb (2.5 kg) chicken backs and necks

1 leek, including about 6 inches (15 cm)
of the green tops, coarsely chopped

2 carrots, coarsely chopped

1 rib celery, coarsely chopped

12 fresh flat-leaf parsley stems

1 sprig fresh thyme

8–10 black peppercorns

MAKES ABOUT 3 QT (3 L)

In a stockpot or large, heavy pot, combine the chicken backs and necks, leek, carrots, celery, parsley, thyme, and peppercorns. Add cold water to cover by 1 inch (2.5 cm).

Place the pot over medium-high heat and slowly bring almost to a boil. Using a large spoon, skim off any scum and froth from the surface. Reduce the heat to low and simmer, uncovered, skimming the surface as needed and adding more water if necessary to keep the ingredients immersed, until the meat has fallen off the bones and the stock is fragrant and flavorful, about 3 hours.

Remove from the heat and let stand until the liquid is almost at room temperature, about 1 hour. Using a slotted spoon or skimmer, lift out the large solids and discard. Pour the stock through a fine-mesh sieve into a storage container with a tight-fitting lid, and discard the solids from the sieve.

Let the stock cool to room temperature, then cover and refrigerate until chilled. Using a spoon, lift off the congealed layer of fat on top and discard. Refrigerate the stock for up to 5 days or freeze for up to 2 months.

Roasted Tomato Sauce

1½ lb (750 g) plum tomatoes, cored

1 small white onion, sliced

2 cloves garlic, unpeeled

1½ tsp olive oil

Salt

MAKES 1¼ CUPS (10 FL OZ/310 ML)

Line a heavy frying pan with aluminum foil and place over medium-high heat. Put the tomatoes, onion, and garlic in the pan and roast, turning occasionally, until the flesh is soft and the skins are charred, about 5 minutes for the garlic and 10–15 minutes for the tomatoes and onion. Peel the garlic and process all the vegetables in a food processor until smooth, adding up to ½ cup (4 fl oz/125 ml) water if needed.

In a frying pan over medium-high heat, warm the oil. Pour in the tomato mixture and stir for 2 minutes. Reduce the heat to medium-low and cook until the sauce thickens, 15–20 minutes. Season with salt. Use as directed in the recipe, or let cool, cover, and refrigerate for up to 5 days or freeze for up to 2 months.

Classic Tomato Sauce

4 tbsp (2 oz/60 g) unsalted butter

2 carrots, finely chopped

1 small rib celery, finely chopped

1 small yellow onion, finely chopped

2 lb (1 kg) fresh plum tomatoes, peeled, seeded (page 290), and chopped, or 1 can (28 oz/875 g) plum tomatoes, drained and chopped

Salt and freshly ground pepper

MAKES ABOUT 4 CUPS (32 FL OZ/1 L)

In a large frying pan over medium heat, melt the butter. Add the carrots, celery, and onion and cook, stirring occasionally, until the vegetables are very tender, about 15 minutes. Add the tomatoes, 1 tsp salt, and a pinch of pepper and cook until the sauce begins to bubble. Reduce the heat to low and cook, stirring occasionally, until the sauce has thickened and the tomato juices have evaporated,

about 1 hour. Taste and adjust the seasoning. For a chunkier sauce, remove from the heat and use as is; for a smoother sauce, use an immersion blender or transfer the sauce to a food processor to purée the sauce to the desired consistency. Use as directed immediately, or let cool, cover, and refrigerate in an airtight container for up to 5 days or freeze for up to 2 months.

Red Chile Sauce

10 ancho chiles, seeded and torn into large pieces

Boiling water

1 can (14¼ oz/455 g) diced tomatoes, with juice

½ white onion, coarsely chopped

6 cloves garlic

1 tsp dried oregano

½ cup (4 fl oz/125 ml) chicken stock, homemade (page 283) or purchased, or as needed

MAKES ABOUT 2 CUPS (16 FL OZ/500 ML)

Put the chiles in a pot and add boiling water to cover. Weight the chiles down with a plate and let soak until soft, about 15 minutes. Drain. In batches, in a blender or food processor, process the chiles, tomatoes with juice, onion, garlic, and oregano until smooth, adding stock as needed to achieve a very smooth consistency. Use as directed in the recipe.

Salsa Fresca

2 plum tomatoes, seeded (page 290) and finely chopped

¼ white onion, finely chopped

2 tbsp minced fresh cilantro

Salt

MAKES ABOUT ¾ CUP (4½ OZ/140 G)

In a bowl, combine the tomatoes, onion, cilantro, and ½ tsp salt and stir to mix well. Taste and add more salt, if needed. Use as directed in the recipe.

PICO DE GALLO VARIATION Add 1 serrano or jalapeño chile, minced with its seeds, and fresh lime juice to taste to the salsa fresca.

Tomatillo-Avocado Salsa

12 tomatillos

3 serrano chiles, seeded and coarsely chopped

½ white onion, cut into small chunks

¾ cup (1 oz/30 g) minced fresh cilantro,
plus whole leaves for garnish

1 tsp dark brown sugar

2 avocados, halved and pitted

Salt

MAKES ABOUT 3 CUPS (24 FL OZ/750 ML)

Remove the papery husks from the tomatillos, rinse, and chop coarsely. In a blender or food processor, combine the chiles, onion, and ½ cup (4 fl oz/125 ml) water. Process until partially smooth. Add the tomatillos, minced cilantro, and brown sugar and blend until the mixture forms a coarse purée.

Scoop the avocados into a bowl and mash coarsely with a fork. Stir in the chile sauce and season to taste with salt. Garnish with the cilantro leaves and use as directed.

Chipotle Chile Salsa

2 ripe tomatoes, about 1 lb (500 g)

2 cloves garlic, unpeeled

3 canned chipotle chiles in adobo sauce

Salt

MAKES ABOUT 1 CUP (8 FL OZ/250 ML)

Line a heavy frying pan with aluminum foil and place over medium-high heat. Put the tomatoes and garlic in the pan and roast, turning occasionally, until the flesh is soft and the skins are charred, about 5 minutes for the garlic and 10–15 minutes for the tomatoes.

Scrape off some of the adobo sauce from the chiles and put them in a blender or food processor. Peel the roasted garlic and chop the tomatoes, then add them to the blender and process briefly. The mixture should be thick and slightly chunky. Pour into a bowl, season to taste with salt, cover, and let stand at room temperature for about 30 minutes to blend the flavors. Taste and add more salt, if needed. Use as directed in the recipe.

Pesto

1½ cups (1½ oz/45 g) lightly packed fresh basil leaves

3 tbsp pine nuts

1 clove garlic, chopped

Salt

⅓ cup (3 fl oz/80 ml) olive oil

¼ lb (125 g) Parmesan cheese, freshly grated

MAKES ABOUT ½ CUP (4 FL OZ/125 ML)

In a large mortar, combine the basil, pine nuts, garlic, and ½ tsp salt. Using a pestle, and working in a circular motion, grind the ingredients together until a thick green paste forms. This can take several minutes. Slowly drizzle in the olive oil while stirring continuously with the pestle until a thick sauce forms. Transfer to a bowl and stir in the cheese. Taste and adjust the seasoning.

Alternatively, in a food processor or blender, process the basil, pine nuts, garlic, and ½ tsp salt until finely chopped. Then, with the motor running, pour in the oil in a slow, steady stream and process until a thick sauce forms. Transfer to a bowl and stir in the cheese. Taste and adjust the seasoning. Use as directed in the recipe.

Chile-Lime Dipping Sauce

1 red Fresno chile, seeded and chopped

3 cloves garlic, minced

1 tbsp sugar

¼ cup (2 fl oz/60 ml) fish sauce

3 tbsp fresh lime juice

1 tbsp rice vinegar

½ small carrot, grated

1 small Thai chile, thinly sliced into rings

MAKES ⅓ CUP (3 FL OZ/80 ML)

In a mini food processor or mortar, combine the Fresno chile, garlic, and sugar and process or grind with a pestle until a smooth paste forms. Transfer the chile paste to a bowl and stir in the fish sauce, lime juice, vinegar, and 2 tbsp warm water. Garnish with the grated carrot and sliced Thai chile. Use as directed in the recipe.

Spicy Thai Dressing

1 tbsp chopped shallot

2 cloves garlic, chopped

1 tbsp seeded and minced jalapeño chile

1 tsp sugar

Freshly ground pepper

¼ cup (2 fl oz/60 ml) fish sauce

¼ cup (2 fl oz/60 ml) fresh lime juice

1 tbsp rice vinegar

1 tsp chile-garlic sauce such as Sriracha

3 tbsp canola oil

MAKES ABOUT ¾ CUP (6 FL OZ/180 ML)

In a mini food processor or mortar, combine the shallot, garlic, chile, sugar, and ⅛ tsp pepper and process or grind with a pestle until a smooth paste forms. Add 1–2 tsp water if needed to facilitate the grinding. Transfer the garlic paste to a bowl and whisk in the fish sauce, lime juice, vinegar, and chile-garlic sauce. Gradually drizzle in the oil while continuing to whisk. Use as directed in the recipe.

Thai Red Curry Paste

2 red Fresno chiles, seeded and chopped

3 cloves garlic, chopped

2 shallots, chopped

1 tbsp chopped fresh ginger

1 lemongrass stalk, white part only, chopped

1 tbsp chopped cilantro stems

1 tbsp ground coriander

1 tsp ground cumin

½ tsp shrimp paste (optional)

MAKES ABOUT ½ CUP (4 OZ/125 G)

In a mini food processor or mortar, combine the chiles, garlic, shallots, ginger, lemongrass, cilantro stems, coriander, cumin, and shrimp paste, if using, and process or grind with a pestle until a smooth paste forms.

Add 1–2 tbsp water if needed to facilitate the grinding. Use as directed in the recipe.

Aioli

1–3 cloves garlic

Salt

6 egg yolks, at room temperature

2 cups (16 fl oz/500 ml) light olive oil, or a mixture of canola oil and olive oil

Freshly ground pepper

Fresh lemon juice (optional)

MAKES ABOUT 2 CUPS (16 FL OZ/500 ML)

In a blender, combine the garlic cloves and 1 tsp salt and process until combined. Add the egg yolks and blend well. With the motor running, pour in the oil in a slow, steady stream and blend until the mixture thickens to the consistency of mayonnaise. If the mixture is too thick, thin with a little lemon juice to the desired consistency. Season to taste with pepper. Use as directed in a recipe.

Raita

1 small cucumber

Salt and ground white pepper

1 clove garlic, minced

1 cup (8 oz/250 g) plain yogurt

2 tbsp fresh lemon juice

½ tsp ground cumin

2 tbsp minced fresh cilantro leaves

MAKES 1½ CUPS (12 OZ/375 G)

Peel the cucumber, then slice it in half lengthwise and scoop out the seeds and pulp with a teaspoon. Finely chop the flesh. Place the chopped cucumber in a fine-mesh sieve, sprinkle with 1 tsp salt, and toss to mix well. Set aside and let drain for 30 minutes at room temperature. Pat the cucumber dry with paper towels.

In a mortar or on a cutting board, using a pestle or the side of a chef's knife, grind or mash the minced garlic with ½ tsp salt to form a smooth paste.

In a bowl, combine the garlic paste, yogurt, lemon juice, cumin, cilantro, and ⅛ tsp white pepper. Fold in the cucumber. Taste and adjust the seasoning. Use as directed in the recipe.

Indian Yogurt Marinade

1 cup (8 oz/250 g) plain yogurt

1 tbsp fresh lemon juice

2 tbsp grated fresh ginger

3 cloves garlic, minced

1 tsp *each* garam masala and salt

½ tsp *each* ground cumin, ground coriander, and ground turmeric

⅛ tsp cayenne pepper

MAKES 1 CUP (8 OZ/250 G)

In a large bowl, combine the yogurt, lemon juice, ginger, garlic, garam masala, salt, cumin, coriander, turmeric, and cayenne and stir to mix well. Use as directed in the recipe.

Tandoori Marinade

1 cup (8 oz/250 g) plain yogurt

⅓ cup (1½ oz/45 g) chopped yellow onion

1–2 serrano chiles, thinly sliced

1 tbsp grated fresh ginger

1 large clove garlic, thinly sliced

7 or 8 large fresh mint leaves, chopped

1 tsp *each* ground cumin, ground coriander, Hungarian sweet paprika, and garam masala

½ tsp ground turmeric

Freshly ground pepper

MAKES 1⅓ CUPS (10 OZ/315 G)

In a blender or food processor, combine the yogurt, onion, chiles, ginger, garlic, mint, cumin, coriander, paprika, garam masala, turmeric, and ¼ tsp pepper and process until smooth. Use as directed in the recipe.

Cooked Fresh Spinach

Fresh spinach leaves, stemmed if large

YIELD VARIES

Rinse the spinach carefully in 2 or 3 changes of water, discarding the tough stems and any damaged leaves. Drain briefly in a colander and then, working in batches if necessary, transfer to a large saucepan with only the water that clings to the leaves. Place over medium-high heat, cover, and cook, turning the leaves a few times, until wilted and slightly firm to the bite, 5–6 minutes. Drain well and chop. Squeeze the spinach with your hands to remove most of the moisture. Use as directed.

Cooked Fresh Fava Beans

Fresh fava beans in the pod

YIELD VARIES

Working with one pod at a time, tear off the stem end. Use your thumb to split open the pod along its seam, and push out each of the fava beans inside. Very young, tender fava beans may be eaten without removing the fuzzy skin, but most must be peeled. Bring a saucepan of water to a boil, add the fava beans, and cook for 1 minute to loosen the skins. Drain and let cool under running water. Use your fingertips to pinch each bean and pop it out of its skin. Use a paring knife to help peel any stubborn ones. Serve the beans or use as directed.

Cooked Dried Beans

1 cup (7 oz/220 g) dried beans, picked over and rinsed

Salt and freshly ground pepper

MAKES 2½–3 CUPS (18–21 OZ/560–655 G)

Place the beans in a large bowl with cold water to cover by about 3 inches (7.5 cm) and let soak for at least 4 hours or up to overnight. (Alternatively, transfer the rinsed beans to a large pot, add water to cover by 3 inches, bring to a boil, remove from the heat, and let stand for 1–2 hours.)

Drain the beans, place in saucepan with cold water to cover by about 4 inches (10 cm), and bring to a boil over high heat, skimming off the foam that rises to the surface. Reduce the heat to low, cover partially, and simmer until the beans are tender, 1½–2½ hours. The timing will depend on the variety and age of the beans.

Steamed Rice

2 cups (14 oz/440 g) basmati, jasmine, sticky, or other long-grain white rice

MAKES 4 CUPS (20 OZ/625 G)

Place the rice in a fine-mesh sieve and rinse under running cold water. Drain.

Transfer the rice to a 2- to 3-qt (2- to 3-l) heavy saucepan and add 3 cups (24 fl oz/750 ml) water. Bring to a boil over medium heat, stir once, and then reduce the heat to low. Cover the pan with a tight-fitting lid and cook the rice, undisturbed, for 20 minutes. Remove from the heat and let stand, covered, for 10 minutes. Fluff the rice with a fork before serving.

To use a rice cooker, rinse and drain the rice as directed, then place in the rice cooker bowl with 3 cups water and cook according to the manufacturer's instructions. Serve.

Coconut Rice

1 tbsp canola oil

1 large shallot, minced

1 tsp minced fresh ginger

2 cups (14 oz/440 g) jasmine rice, rinsed

1 cup (8 fl oz/250 ml) coconut milk

Salt

3 lemongrass stalks, tender midsections only

MAKES 4–6 SERVINGS

In a large saucepan over medium-high heat, warm the oil. Add the shallot and ginger and sauté until fragrant, about 30 seconds. Add the rice to the pan and stir to mix well. Add 2 cups (16 fl oz/500 ml) water, the coconut milk, and 1 tsp salt and bring to a boil. Reduce the heat to low. Smash the lemongrass with the heel of your hand against the side of a chef's knife and stir into the rice. Cover and simmer for 20 minutes.

Remove the pan from the heat and let the rice stand, covered, until tender, about 10 minutes longer. Discard the lemongrass stalks and fluff the rice with a fork. Transfer the rice to a warmed bowl and serve.

Herbed Rice Pilaf

2 tbsp olive oil or unsalted butter

2 shallots, minced

1 cup (7 oz/220 g) long-grain white rice

1½ cups (12 fl oz/350 ml) chicken stock, homemade (page 283) or purchased

Salt and freshly ground pepper

¼ cup (⅓ oz/10 g) minced mixed fresh herbs such as marjoram, thyme, tarragon, basil, oregano, mint, and cilantro

MAKES 4 SERVINGS

In a saucepan over medium heat, warm the olive oil. Add the shallots and sauté until softened, 1–2 minutes. Stir in the rice and cook, stirring, until the grains are coated, about 1 minute. Add the stock and ¼ tsp salt. Bring to a boil over high heat. Cover, reduce the heat to low, and simmer gently until the liquid has been absorbed and the rice is tender, about 20 minutes. Remove from the heat.

Sprinkle the herbs over the rice. Do not stir. Re-cover and let stand for 5 minutes. Stir gently to combine the rice and herbs. Season to taste with salt and pepper. Serve.

Shredded Cooked Chicken

2 lb (1 kg) bone-in chicken breasts or thighs

Slice of white onion

4 black peppercorns

1 clove garlic

Salt

MAKES 2 CUPS (12 OZ/375 G)

Place the chicken pieces in a saucepan and add enough water to cover. Place over medium-high heat until the water comes to a boil, skimming off any foam that forms on the surface. Reduce the heat to low and add the onion, peppercorns, and garlic. Cover and simmer gently until the meat is opaque throughout, about 20 minutes. Add salt to taste during the last 5 minutes.

Transfer the chicken to a plate to cool. When cool enough to handle, coarsely shred the chicken, discarding any skin and bones. Use as directed in the recipe.

Quiche Dough

2 cups (10 oz/315 g) flour

½ tsp salt

½ cup (4 oz/125 g) cold unsalted butter, cut into ½-inch (12-mm) pieces

6 tbsp (3 fl oz/90 ml) ice water

MAKES ONE 9-INCH (23-CM) QUICHE

Put the flour and salt in a food processor and process to combine. Scatter the butter pieces over the flour mixture. Process with short pulses just until pea-sized crumbs form. Add the ice water and pulse briefly until the dough begins to clump; do not overprocess the dough or it will become tough. Gather together the dough and flatten into a disk. Wrap the dough disk in plastic wrap, and refrigerate for 30 minutes.

On a floured work surface, roll out the dough into a round about 10½ inches (26.5 cm) in diameter and ¼ inch (6 mm) thick. Drape the dough over a rolling pin and carefully transfer it to a 9-inch (23-cm) quiche pan with 1-inch (2.5-cm) sides. Using your fingers, press the dough into the bottom and sides of the pan. Trim any overhanging edges or pinch the dough around the rim to form a fluted edge. Use as directed in the recipe.

Tartlet Dough

1¼ cups (6½ oz/200 g) flour

2 tbsp sugar

¼ tsp salt

6 tbsp (3 oz/90 g) unsalted butter, at room temperature

3 tbsp cold cream cheese

2 tbsp ice water

MAKES TWELVE 3-INCH (7.5-CM) TARTLETS

Whisk together the flour, sugar, and salt. In a large bowl, using a mixer on medium speed, beat the butter and cream cheese until well combined, about 1 minute. Add the dry ingredients and the ice water and beat until the dough forms large clumps. Scrape down the sides of the bowl and then turn the dough out onto a lightly floured work surface. Use as directed in the recipe.

Suzette Butter

Grated zest and juice from 1 orange

½ cup (4 oz/125 g) unsalted butter

⅓ cup (3 oz/90 g) sugar

MAKES ¾ CUP (6 OZ/185 G)

In a food processor, process the orange zest, butter, and sugar until completely blended. With the motor running, slowly add the orange juice and process again until blended. Use as directed in the recipe.

Meringue Frosting

1 cup (8 oz/250 g) sugar

4 large egg whites, at room temperature

¼ tsp cream of tartar

MAKES ENOUGH FROSTING FOR
ONE 9-BY-12-INCH (23-BY-30-CM) CAKE

In a small saucepan, combine the sugar and ½ cup (4 fl oz/125 ml) water and bring to a boil over medium-high heat, stirring to dissolve the sugar. Reduce the heat to medium-low and simmer, washing down the sides of the pan with a pastry brush dipped in cold water.

When the syrup comes to a boil, in a clean metal bowl, combine the egg whites and cream of tartar and, using a mixer on high speed, beat until stiff peaks form. Continue cooking the syrup until a candy thermometer registers 230°F (110°C), 10–12 minutes. Slowly and carefully add the hot syrup to the egg whites while beating, until all the syrup is incorporated. Continue beating until the frosting is cooled and glossy. Use as directed in the recipe.

Whipped Cream

1 cup (8 fl oz/250 ml) heavy cream

1 tbsp sugar

1 tsp pure vanilla extract

MAKES ABOUT 2 CUPS (16 FL OZ/500 ML)

In a large bowl, combine the cream, sugar, and vanilla. Using a balloon whisk or a mixer on medium-high speed, beat until medium peaks form. Use as directed.

Basic Techniques

Toasting Nuts & Coconut

Preheat the oven to 325°F (165°C). Spread the nuts or shredded dried coconut in a single layer on a baking sheet and toast, stirring occasionally for even browning, until they are fragrant and the color deepens. Watch them carefully, as timing varies depending on the type of nut and the size of the pieces. Most nuts will take between 10 and 20 minutes; pine nuts, flaked almonds, and shredded coconut will require just 5–10 minutes.

Zesting & Juicing Citrus

When you need to both zest and juice a lemon, lime, or orange, start by zesting and finish by juicing. To zest, use a citrus zester, rasp grater, vegetable peeler, or paring knife to carefully remove only the colored layer of the rind, avoiding the bitter white pith. Once the fruit is zested, cut it in half and use a citrus reamer or juicer to break the membranes and free the juices. Work over a bowl and strain the juice with a fine-mesh sieve to remove the pulp and seeds.

Peeling & Segmenting Citrus

For some preparations, like salads, you will want to remove all of the peel and pith from the citrus flesh. Start by slicing off the top and bottom of the fruit. To peel the fruit, stand it on its flat bottom and carefully slice off the peel down to the bright flesh, following the contour of the fruit's sides with your knife. To segment the fruit, holding the fruit over a bowl, cut on either side of each segment to free it from the membrane and let the segments fall into the bowl, which will also catch the juices if needed for a dressing or sauce.

Slicing Mango

To dice a mango, see instructions on page 212. To slice a mango, peel it first, using a paring knife or vegetable peeler. Locate the position of the wide, flat pit using the tip of your knife, then carefully hold the slippery fruit upright and slice the flesh from the flat sides of the pits. Place the two mango halves cut side down and slice.

Slicing & Dicing Avocado

To slice an avocado neatly, do it while the flesh is still in the skin. First cut the avocado in half lengthwise, working around the pit. Twist the halves in opposite directions to separate them. Use a spoon to nudge out the pit, or carefully strike the pit with the heel of your knife so the knife lodges in the pit, and lift it out. Slice the avocado flesh, then use a large spoon to carefully scoop it out of the skin, keeping the slices intact. To dice, make crosshatch slices in opposite directions before scooping out the flesh.

Peeling Tomatoes

Some recipes call for peeling and/or seeding tomatoes to create a smooth texture in a sauce or other preparation. To peel tomatoes (or other thin-skinned produce such as peaches), bring a pot of water to a boil. Cut a shallow "X" in the bottom of each tomato, then slip the tomatoes into the boiling water. After 15–30 seconds, depending on ripeness, the skins will wrinkle. Remove the tomatoes with a slotted spoon and transfer them to a bowl of ice water to stop the cooking. When the tomatoes have cooled slightly, use a paring knife or your fingers to pull off the peels, starting at the "X."

Seeding Tomatoes

The technique for seeding a tomato is slightly different depending on the type of tomato. To seed globe tomatoes, cut the tomatoes in half crosswise through the "equator." Cut plum or Roma tomatoes in half lengthwise. Holding a tomato half over a bowl, use a finger to scoop out the seed sacs and any excess liquid. You can also squeeze the tomato half gently to push out the seeds.

Roasting Tomatoes

To roast tomatoes, line a heavy frying pan with heavy-duty aluminum foil and heat over medium-high heat. Put the tomatoes in the pan and roast them, turning occasionally, until the skins are blackened and the interiors of the tomatoes have softened, 10–15 minutes. The most blackened parts of the tomato skins can be removed before using.

Seeding & Deveining Chiles

If your skin is sensitive, wear disposable latex gloves when working with chiles, and avoid touching your eyes or mouth. Using a paring knife, trim away the stem. Cut the chile in half lengthwise, then into quarters. Cut away the seeds and membranes from each chile quarter. Capsaicin, the compound that makes chiles hot, is concentrated in these areas; removing them lessens the heat. If you want more spice, leave some of the seeds.

Roasting Fresh Peppers & Chiles

You can roast peppers and chiles on the stove top, on a grill, or under a broiler. For the stove top method, using tongs, place the peppers or chiles directly over the flame of a gas stove. Turn often until the skin is charred and blistered, 2–3 minutes. For the grill method, place peppers and chiles on a gas or charcoal grill as close to the hot fire as possible until the skin is charred and blistered, 3–5 minutes. For the broil method, place peppers or chiles on a foil-lined pan, and broil as close to the heat source as possible, turning them often, until blackened, 5–10 minutes.

TO REMOVE THE SKIN After roasting, place the peppers or chiles in a paper or heavy-duty plastic bag and let stand for about 8 minutes to help loosen the skin. This will also soften the flesh, so do not leave them too long. Pick and peel away as much skin as possible. Do not worry if some charred bits remain.

TO SEED If stuffing the pepper or chile, using a small knife, slit each chile lengthwise from the stem area to the bottom, leaving ½ inch (12 mm) uncut on top and at least ¼ inch (6 mm) on the bottom. Leaving the stem intact, remove the seeds and membranes with your fingers. Wipe the inside of the pepper or chile with a damp towel, checking to see that all the seeds and membranes are removed. Dry well. For slicing or chopping, slit the pepper or chile lengthwise and spread it out. Cut out the stem, then remove the seeds and membranes.

Cleaning Leeks

As leeks grow, dirt is sometimes trapped among their many layers. To clean a leek thoroughly, trim off the dark green leaves and most but not all of the root end, then slice the stalk in half lengthwise. Rinse the both halves well under running cold water, separating the layers with your fingers and making sure all the dirt is removed.

Cleaning Mushrooms

Avoid soaking mushrooms, so that they do not become waterlogged and add extra moisture to your cooked dish. Clean mushrooms with a soft brush or dampened paper towel, simply brushing or wiping off the dirt. You can also rinse mushrooms; just work quickly so they do not soak up too much water, and drain at once.

Trimming Artichoke Hearts

Fill a bowl three-fourths full with cold water. Squeeze in the juice of ½ lemon. Working with one artichoke at a time, cut off the top ¾ inch (2 cm) of the leaves with a serrated knife to remove the thorny tips. Trim off the tough end of the stem. Pull off the tough, dark green outer leaves until you reach the tenderest, palest green inner leaves. Using a small, sharp knife, peel away the tough, dark outer flesh around the base of the leaves and on the stem. Lay the artichoke on its side and use the serrated knife to cut off the remaining leaves where they meet the top of the base. Using a teaspoon, scoop out the fuzzy choke and soft flesh covering the heart. With the small, sharp knife, trim away any remaining tough parts around the sides and on the bottom of the heart. Drop each artichoke heart into the lemon water, which will slow browning and discoloration.

Cutting Corn Kernels from a Cob

To remove the kernels from an ear of corn, first shuck the ear and remove the flossy corn silk. Make a flat cut through the stem end of the cob so you can stand the ear upright and hold it stable. Stand the ear on a cutting board and, using a sharp chef's knife, slice off the kernels as close to the cob as possible.

Pitting Olives

To remove the pits from olives, use a cherry pitter to punch the pit through the end of the olive. Or, put the olives in a zippered plastic bag, force out the excess air, and seal the bag. Using a meat pounder or a rolling pin, gently pound the olives to loosen the pits. Remove the crushed olives from the bag and separate the pits from the flesh. Use a paring knife to cut out any stubborn pits.

Working with Fresh Ginger

Before slicing, mincing, or grating fresh gingerroot, peel it with a vegetable peeler or the edge of a soup spoon. Refrigerate ginger for up to 2 weeks wrapped in a dry paper towel inside a plastic bag.

Making Ginger Juice

To make ginger juice, peel fresh ginger. Using a ginger grater or a mini food processor, grate or mince the ginger into a bowl. Using your hands, squeeze the grated or minced ginger to extract as much juice as possible, discarding the solids or reserving for another use. Approximately 2 tbsp grated ginger will yield 1 tbsp juice.

Working with Fresh Lemongrass

With their long, flat leaves and woody stems, lemongrass stalks resemble sturdy, pale green onions. To prepare lemongrass, remove the outer layers from the stalk and trim away the green leaves and root end, leaving about 6 inches (15 cm) of the tender, ivory-colored midsection. Lay the lemongrass on a cutting board and bruise by pressing with the heel of your hand against the flat side of a chef's knife, then slice or chop.

Separating Eggs

Eggs are easiest to separate when they are cold. Have ready 2 clean, grease-free bowls, or 3 bowls if you are separating multiple eggs. Crack an egg sharply on a flat surface, then hold the cracked egg over an empty bowl and carefully pull the shell apart into two halves, letting the white (but not the yolk) start to drop into the bowl. Pass the yolk back and forth from one shell half to the other, letting the remaining white fall into the bowl. Be careful not to break the yolk on the sharp eggshell edge. Place the yolk in a separate bowl. If you are separating more eggs, pour the white into the third bowl and separate each new egg over an empty bowl. This way, if a yolk breaks and mixes with the white, it will not mix with all the egg whites. If you are planning to whip your egg whites, just a trace of egg yolk or another fat will prevent them from whipping up. If an egg does not separate well, use it for scrambled eggs or an omelet.

Hard-Boiling Eggs

Place the eggs in a saucepan and add cold water to cover by 1 inch (2.5 cm). Bring just to a boil, then remove the pan from the heat and cover. Let the eggs stand in the hot water for 15 minutes. Using a slotted spoon, remove the eggs. Pour off the hot water and fill the pan with cold water. Return the eggs to the pan and let cool for about 5 minutes, and then remove the eggs and peel them under running cold water, or refrigerate for up to 1 week. Note that hard-boiled eggs with a gray-green ring around the yolks have been overcooked.

Peeling Shrimp

If the heads are attached, grasp the head of each shrimp in one hand and the tail in the other and twist apart. Pull off the legs on the underside. Starting with the section of shell closest to the head, pull it up and lift it away. As you pull away the first section of shell, it will bring the other overlapping sections with it. For some recipes, you may wish to leave the final tail section of the shrimp intact. If you do remove it, give the tip of the tail a squeeze as you pull to release the meat.

Deveining Shrimp

Make a shallow cut along the outer curve almost to the tail of the shrimp. You may or may not clearly see a dark vein running through the meat. This is the intestinal tract of the shrimp. It is removed for appearance's sake and because it can contribute an unpleasant gritty texture. With the tip of the knife, lift out the vein and pull it away, gently scraping it if necessary. Once you have deveined all your shrimp, put them in a colander and rinse with cold water to remove any residual grit.

Butterflying & Halving Chicken

A whole chicken sometimes cooks more quickly and evenly when butterflied, or opened flat. Place the chicken on a cutting board with the breast side down. Using poultry shears or a large, sharp, heavy knife, cut through the bone along one side of the backbone. Pull the bird open slightly and cut along the other side of the backbone to free it. (Reserve the backbone for making stock, or discard it.) Turn the chicken breast side up and open it as flat as possible. Press firmly with the heel of your hand to break the breastbone and flatten the chicken. To halve the chicken, use the shears to cut the bird in half through the breastbone. Trim away any excess skin or clumps of fat.

Cutting a Chicken into Pieces

To divide a whole bird into serving pieces, use poultry shears to cut through the skin between each thigh and the body. Bend the leg back to loosen the thighbone from its joint, then cut through it to remove the entire leg. To separate the thigh from the drumstick, locate the joint by following the thin line of fat between them. Cut through the joint to separate the pieces. Turn the bird's body to access each wing. Move each wing to locate the joint connecting it to the body, and then cut through the joint to free the wing. Cut along both sides of the backbone and remove it. Cut through the center of the breast to split it in half, and if desired cut each breast crosswise into 2 pieces. Prepared in this manner, a whole chicken will yield 8 to 10 pieces. For 12 pieces, cut each thigh in half crosswise.

Charcoal Grilling

Ignite the coals using a chimney starter. When they are white, dump them into the grill. If needed, add unlit coals.

FOR DIRECT-HEAT GRILLING Heap the coals on one side of the grill to make a hotter zone, and leave at least one-third of the fire bed free of coals. Position the grill rack in its slots over the coals. Be sure the grill rack is well oiled before placing food on it, to prevent sticking.

FOR INDIRECT-HEAT GRILLING Arrange the lit coals into 2 equal piles on either side of the fire bed and place a foil drip pan in the center, leaving the middle of the grill without heat. Pour water into the pan and position the grill rack with its handles over the coals. For even cooking, tie or truss the food into a compact shape. Put the food on the center of the grill rack directly over the drip pan and cover the grill.

TO TEST THE HEAT LEVEL Hold your hand as long as you can 4 inches (10 cm) above the coals: 1 or 2 seconds means a hot fire; 3 or 4 seconds is medium.

Gas Grilling

Turn the fuel valve on the propane tank so that it is all the way open. Turn on all heat elements to the high heat setting. Light the grill by depressing the automatic spark igniter. Close the grill lid and let the bed of lava rock, ceramic briquettes, or metal baffles heat until the temperature in the covered grill reaches at least 350°F (180°C). This will take 10–15 minutes. When ready to cook, turn the knobs to the desired heat level.

FOR DIRECT-HEAT GRILLING To create heat zones, after the grill has preheated, turn down the heat in one-third of the grill, and turn off the heat in another one-third of the grill. You will now have one area with medium to high heat, one area with lower heat, and one area without heat. Place the food to be cooked directly over the higher heat and move it to lower heat as needed to prevent burning.

FOR INDIRECT-HEAT GRILLING After preheating the grill, turn off the heat on one side of the grill and leave the other side turned on. Place the food to be cooked on the unlit side and close the grill lid.

Glossary

BLACK VINEGAR This thick, glossy, dark Asian vinegar has a complex flavor with a hint of wood smoke. You can substitute balsamic vinegar, which has a similar flavor.

BROCCOLI RABE A relative of turnip greens, broccoli rabe, also known as rapini or rape, has dark green leafy stems topped by clusters of broccoli-like florets. Remove any tough stems and wilted leaves before cooking. If the lower parts of the stalks are fibrous, cut them away.

CHILE BEAN PASTE When fermented and puréed with chiles, garlic, and spices, soybeans create a strong, thick, salty-hot paste that gives bold flavor to Chinese dishes.

CHILE-GARLIC SAUCE Named for a town in the south of Thailand, Sriracha is a bright red, smoothly textured chile-garlic sauce. Its hint of sweetness makes it a versatile ingredient and popular condiment.

CHILE OIL This clear, red oil infused with the spicy heat of dried chiles is especially popular as a condiment in China. Some versions include flakes of roasted chile, black beans, or toasted sesame oil for richer flavor.

CHILE PASTE Many different types of pastes made from chiles are used throughout China and Southeast Asia. They range from thin pastes made of fresh chiles to thick pastes ground from dried or pungently fermented chiles. Salt or vinegar may be added as a preservative, and other ingredients such as garlic, dried shrimp, tamarind, fried shallots, or grated ginger contribute multiple layers of flavor and texture.

CHILES AND PEPPERS Hundreds of chile varieties thrive around the world and are especially favored in the Mediterranean, Asia, and Latin America:

Ancho A mild, dark reddish brown or brick red, squat-looking dried poblano chile. About 4 inches (10 cm) long, anchos can pack a bit of heat along with their natural sweetness. Ancho chile powder is available in Latin markets and is generally considered to make the best pure ground chile powder. Use California chiles or mulato chiles when anchos are not available.

Chipotle The smoke-dried form of the ripened jalapeño, this chile is rich in flavor and very hot. It is typically a leathery brown to deep burgundy. Chipotles are also widely sold canned in adobo sauce.

Fresno A mild to hot chile that is about 3 inches (7.5 cm) long and less fleshy than the jalapeño.

Habanero One of the hottest of all chiles, this 2-inch (5-cm) lantern-shaped variety combines its intense heat with flavors of tomatoes and tropical fruits. Available in unripe green and ripe yellow, orange, and red forms.

Jalapeño A popular fresh chile that can range from mild to fiery hot. The thick-walled jalapeño tapers 2–4 inches (5–10 cm) to a blunt tip and is usually green in color, although riper, sweeter red chiles are seasonally available.

Piquillo A fire-roasted mild red pepper from the Navarra region of Spain, sold in glass jars.

Poblano This tapered, moderately hot chile is about 5 inches (13 cm) long and a polished deep green.

Red, Dried These thin, pointed, bright red chiles are similar to dried árbol and cayenne chiles, which can be substituted. To lessen their heat, trim the stem and shake out the seeds.

Serrano This fresh chile up to 2 inches (5 cm) long is sold in its green or ripened red form. Green serranos in particular tend to be hot.

Thai These small, pointy green or red chiles are very hot. Milder serrano or jalapeño may be substituted.

CHORIZO The name refers both to well-seasoned links of fresh pork sausage from Mexico and dry-cured pork sausage from Spain. Mexican chorizo is the spicier of the two and needs to be cooked.

COCONUT Growing on palm trees in tropical climates, the coconut is the world's largest nut.

Coconut Cream Rich in natural fats, coconut cream rises to the top of the coconut milk when undisturbed. To settle coconut cream for measuring, place an unopened can of coconut milk in the refrigerator and let stand for at least 4 hours. Open the can, being careful not to shake it. The cream will be floating in a solid layer on top of the milk. Spoon out the amount of cream required, transfer any unused coconut milk or cream to a clean container, and refrigerate for up to 1 week. Do not confuse this unsweetened coconut cream with the small cans of sweetened coconut cream used for making mixed drinks.

Coconut Milk Pressed from the grated meat of the ripened nut, coconut milk lends sweetness and richness to sauces, soups, desserts, and drinks. Shake canned coconut milk well before adding to recipes.

Coconut Water Not to be confused with coconut milk, coconut water is the clear liquid found inside of a fresh coconut. It can be found in most well-stocked markets.

CUCUMBERS English, or hothouse, cucumbers are nearly seedless, 12–16 inches (30–40 cm) long, and have a thin, smooth, edible skin. Other cucumbers should be peeled and seeded. To seed, slice the cucumber in half lengthwise and scoop out the seeds and pulp with a teaspoon.

CURRY POWDER In India, dried spices are roasted, ground, and then blended into complex mixes, known as *masalas,* to flavor sauces. In the West, prepackaged "Madras" curry powder is a commonly available mixture that is brightly colored yellow with turmeric.

FERMENTED BLACK BEANS This staple of Chinese pantries is made from dried soybeans that have been fermented until black in color and slightly soft in texture. Some versions are flavored with aromatics such as anise or tangerine peel. Before using, rinse and drain well.

FILO Large, paper-thin sheets of dough, also known as phyllo, create flaky layers of pastry for savory and sweet Middle Eastern and Greek dishes. Freshly made filo is sold in Middle Eastern markets; packages of frozen filo are available in most supermarkets. When working with filo, bring it to room temperature and work quickly, covering the sheets to prevent them from drying out.

FISH SAUCE Salted and packed in large vats, anchovies give off an amber, pungently flavored liquid known as fish sauce. One of the most important seasonings in Southeast Asia, fish sauce is used much like soy sauce as a basic seasoning for meat, poultry, and seafood.

FIVE-SPICE POWDER This classic Chinese spice mixture is an aromatic blend of ground fennel, cloves, cinnamon, Sichuan peppercorns, and star anise.

GARAM MASALA A dried spice mixture essential to Indian cooking, garam masala typically includes cinnamon, fenugreek, cumin, peppercorns, and cardamom. It appears in curries throughout India and Southeast Asia. Cooks also sprinkle it as a finishing spice on dishes just before serving.

GHEE This clarified butter is used in many Indian dishes. It is clarified by gently simmering unsalted butter to remove all of its moisture. The process of clarifying gives the ghee an amber color and unique, nutty flavor. It also increases its smoke point. It can be found in most ethnic markets and well-stocked supermarkets.

HERBES DE PROVENCE This blend of herbs that grow wild on the dry, rocky hillsides of southern France adds a distinctive rustic flavor to roast meats. The mixture usually contains lavender, thyme, basil, fennel seed, and savory, and sometimes marjoram, oregano, and rosemary.

HOISIN SAUCE This popular thick, dark sauce flavored with five-spice powder is a classic Chinese table condiment and is also used in cooking.

KAFFIR LIME LEAVES With their distinctive double leaves and knobby-skinned fruit, kaffir lime trees grow throughout the tropical regions of South and Southeast Asia. The leaves contribute a flowery aroma when simmered whole in stocks and sauces. If the leaves are large, gently tear out the center spine of each leaf.

LENTILS These small legumes come in a wide range of colors, including brown, green, yellow, red, and pink. Red or yellow lentils are a common addition to Indian soups and curries; they cook relatively quickly and break down nicely, becoming a natural thickener.

MUNG BEAN SPROUTS Crisp, white mung bean sprouts contribute freshness and texture to many Asian dishes, especially soups, salads, stir-fried noodles, and rolls. To keep them fresh, immerse in a container of cold water and store in the refrigerator for up to 3 days.

NOODLES, ASIAN Eaten as often as rice in many Asian countries, noodles come in a range of styles:

Cellophane Also known as mung bean, bean thread, or glass noodles, these translucent, firm noodles hold up well to braising and stir-frying. Soak in warm water for 30 minutes and drain before using.

Chinese Egg A wide range of fresh and dried noodles are made from wheat and eggs, from thin threads to wide, flat ribbons.

Rice Especially popular in southern China and Southeast Asia, thin vermicelli and wider rice noodles, available both fresh and dried, have a delicate texture that is enjoyed in brothy soups. Silky ribbons cut from fresh rice noodle sheets are stir-fried or simply steamed.

OYSTER SAUCE A staple in Cantonese cooking, this thick, dark brown sauce was traditionally made from oysters, water, and salt. The sauce's salty-sweet flavor adds richness to braises and stir-fry sauces, and the sauce appears often at Chinese tables as a simple topping for vegetables.

PANCETTA This Italian unsmoked bacon is made from a flat cut of belly pork that is cured with salt and a selection of spices that may include black pepper, cinnamon, clove, nutmeg, or juniper berries, and then rolled into a cylinder for air drying. When the cylinder is cut, the slices display a distinctive spiral of lean, satiny meat and pure, white fat.

PAPRIKA, SPANISH SMOKED Spanish paprika, made from smoked, ground pimiento peppers, has a brick red color and complex, smoky flavor that gives depth and dimension to many Mediterranean dishes.

PRESERVED LEMON A hallmark of Moroccan cooking, preserved lemons are cured in a mixture of salt and their own juice, which turns the rinds soft and the pulp almost jamlike. They can be made at home, or are available in Middle Eastern markets.

PROSCIUTTO This famed Italian ham made from the rear leg of the pig is lightly seasoned, cured with salt, and then air dried. Celebrated for its subtle but intense flavor, prosciutto is eaten raw or is cooked as a flavoring agent. It is almost always used in paper-thin slices. A similar ham that originates in Spain is serrano.

PUFF PASTRY The hundreds of flaky layers in French puff pastry are made by rolling and folding butter into dough, which takes more time and patience than skill. Fortunately, commercial puff pastry dough may be found in the freezer case in well-stocked grocery stores.

QUESO AÑEJO *Queso fresco,* a Mexican fresh cheese, is pressed in a mold to increase density and aged to create *queso añejo.* The aging process gives the cheese a saltier flavor and a medium sharpness. Substitute Parmesan.

RADICCHIO Pleasantly astringent, bitter, and crisp, this prized member of the chicory family is found in several varieties. The most familiar types are compact, round heads of white-ribbed burgundy leaves. They are best used raw in salads. In autumn, the less bitter Treviso type appears in markets. The long, narrow leaves, sometimes red with white ribs or light green with red tips, are enjoyed raw in salads as well, but are also well suited to cooked dishes, such as risotto.

RICE Rice is categorized according to the length of its grains. Long-grain rice, which grows well in warmer climates, has dry, elongated grains when cooked; many varieties are famous for their nutty or floral aromas. Medium- and short-grain rice, which thrive in colder climates, have shorter, plumper grains that cook up moist and glossy. Here are a few particular types:

Arborio The plump, oval, medium-sized grains of this Italian rice are rich in the surface starch that produces risotto's distinctive creamy character. Arborio may be substituted for Bomba and Calasparra, two Spanish rices traditionally used to make paella.

Basmati A long-grain rice with a sweet, nutlike taste and perfume, grown primarily in India, Iran, and the United States, basmati is ideal for use in pilafs. Brown and white varieties are available.

Jasmine Cultivated in Thailand and also in the United States, this long-grain rice variety has a sweet floral scent.

Sticky Also known as sweet or glutinous rice, varieties of this rice include both long and short grain as well as a range of colors from white to red to black. The extra-starchy rice is often used for desserts and fillings.

RICE-PAPER WRAPPERS Rice-paper wrappers are thin, dried sheets that, when moistened, become translucent wrappers. They come in large and small rounds and can be found in most Asian markets.

RICE VINEGAR This mildly flavored vinegar, most often made now from rice wine lees, is widely used in China. Less acidic and sharp than distilled white vinegar, it blends well into salads and light sauces. Depending on the region and the brand, it may range from crystal clear to pale gold in color, with the latter generally having more flavor. Avoid varieties with salt or other flavorings, and look instead for unseasoned rice vinegars.

RICE WINE A spirit distilled from glutinous rice, Chinese rice wine adds depth to marinades, sauces, soups, and classic red-cooked braises. Substitute sake or good-quality dry sherry.

ROSE WATER In India, where it is a favorite ingredient, this dilute distillation of red rose petals lends its flowery fragrance to many desserts and drinks. Orange flower water or a small amount of pure almond extract may be used in its place.

SESAME OIL, ASIAN With its dark amber color and its rich, nutty flavor, this oil pressed from roasted sesame seeds serves as a key ingredient in Chinese food. Not to be confused with the clear, refined sesame oil often used for high-heat cooking, roasted sesame oil is best used in small amounts in marinades, fillings, dipping sauces, and dressings where its flavor can be appreciated.

SHIITAKE MUSHROOMS Also often known as Chinese black mushrooms, brown, flat-capped shiitakes are typically cultivated on oak logs. The stems are tough and should be discarded. The mushrooms are widely available both fresh and dried. The latter, much appreciated for their smoky, meaty flavor and chewy texture, require reconstituting before use.

SHRIMP PASTE Similar to anchovies, shrimp paste is made from salted, fermented, and ground shrimp, the pungent flavor of which lends complex flavor to savory dishes throughout Southeast Asia. Shrimp paste can vary widely from a moist, light gray paste to a dark brown, solid, dry brick.

SOY SAUCE A fundamental seasoning in Asia, soy sauce is a dark, salty liquid made from soy beans fermented with a small amount of wheat to develop complex, meaty flavors. The highest-quality soy sauces are made from only whole beans, wheat, and water and then are aged in barrels. Different types of soy sauces include light soy (not to be confused with "lite" or reduced-sodium soy sauce), the basic version stocked in most Chinese kitchens for its lighter color and saltier flavor, and dark soy, a darker version often used in braises, glazes, and heartier sauces.

TAMARIND PASTE The long fruit pods of the tamarind tree are a staple of India and Southeast Asia. Tamarind is most commonly available puréed into a dark, thick concentrated paste that can be stirred directly into liquids and sauces for a hit of flavor.

THAI BASIL Its purple stems and gentle anise flavor distinguish Thai basil from Italian sweet basil. Popular in Thailand and Vietnam, whole leaves garnish soups, curries, and spicy stir-fries.

TOFU Delicate, creamy, and nutritious bean curd, or tofu, is made by boiling and straining soybeans to make soy milk, then coagulating the milk. The many varieties fall into two different styles: a silken Japanese version and a more coarsely textured Chinese tofu. Silken tofu is best highlighted in soups and appetizers. Firm, extra-firm, and pressed tofu can be cut into cubes and stir-fried, or crumbled and mixed into fillings. Store tofu immersed in a container of cold water. Refrigerate for up to 1 week, changing the water daily.

TOMATILLOS Like the tomato, the tomatillo is a member of the nightshade family. It is covered with a parchment-like husk, which is removed. The fruits, which have a unique texture and tart flavor, are the basis for many cooked sauces and are occasionally used raw in salsas. Carefully rinse off the sticky residue that covers the skin before using.

WONTON WRAPPERS Rolled thinly from a dough of wheat flour, egg, and water and then cut into squares or rounds, wonton wrappers are commonly filled with minced shrimp, pork, tofu, or vegetables. The resulting dumplings can be boiled, steamed, panfried, or deep-fried. Look for them in well-stocked supermarkets.